THE
BEST WEDDING RECEPTION...EVER!
YOUR GUIDE TO CREATING AN UNFORGETTABLY FUN CELEBRATION

PETER MERRY

THE
BEST
WEDDING RECEPTION
...EVER!

YOUR GUIDE TO CREATING
AN
UNFORGETTABLY FUN
CELEBRATION

MERRY WEDDINGS, INC.
LADERA RANCH, CA

PRINTED IN THE UNITED STATES OF AMERICA.

First edition published 2007

    Merry, Peter
       The best wedding reception...ever! : your guide to creating an unforgettably fun celebration / Peter Merry—1st ed.

ISBN 978-1-4243-3178-9

PART III
Adding Your Personal Style
Putting Your Fingerprints on Every Page of Your Reception Plan

acknowledgements

There are so many people to thank for inspiring me, encouraging me and supporting me...but I want to start off by thanking God for creating me and giving me the talents and gifts that have enabled me to provide for my family via my wedding entertainment services.

Next, I have to thank my wife, Lisa, for her tireless support and never-ending belief that this book could actually be completed someday. I'd also like to thank Rick Warren for starting Saddleback Church all those years ago so I could find a church family right when I needed one most. I'd like to thank Mark & Rebecca Ferrell for sharing their insights with me, for opening doors for me, and for telling me I could do it...even when everyone else said it wasn't possible to make a living as a wedding entertainer. I'd like to thank Randy Bartlett for helping me to stay on task and for representing everything that is truly good about being a professional wedding entertainer. I'd like to thank Jim Kennedy for his generosity with the amazing photos featured on the cover and throughout this book. I'd like to thank Brian & Jennifer Varca for allowing me to use their wedding photos on the cover and inside my book. And I'd also like to thank James Loram for not only being a great business partner with Last Dance Entertainment, but also for just being a great friend.

For her invaluable help as my editor, I'd like to thank Amanda Jerome. For their additional editing help, I'd also like to thank Ron Ruth, Melissa Churchwell, Steve Otto, Alex Tamas, Amy Hoekstra, and David Miller.

Thank you, Tom Haibeck, for contributing such a thoughtful foreword and for your generous help with getting my first book printed and promoted.

There are countless entertainers, organizations, and groups to thank in my professional world. Here are just a few of them: The ADJA National Board of Directors, my fellow ADJA members, my Local Southern California ADJA Chapter members, everyone at DiscJockeyAmerica.com, my podcast listeners at DJAradio.com, Ryan Burger and his staff at ProDJ.com, Mobile Beat Magazine & Shows including Mike Buonaccorso & Bob Lindquist, John Young and his staff at the Disc Jockey News and Conferences, members of TT, ABC, NACE, ISES, WMBA, and AFWPI,

Daren Anderson, Andy Austin, Tony Barthel, Cliff Bell, Jon Bruce, Peter Carroll, Jim Cerone, Stuart Chisholm, Mike Connolly, Chris Costa, Alvis Darroch, Ken Day, Jason Diavatis, Wayne Dickson, Tommy Evans, Gary Fernandez, Howard & Leslie Fisher, Bryan Foley, Ed Frank, James Gammell, Brian Graham, Matt Graumann, Dean Hall, Roy Hanschke, Paul Harms, Brian Harris, Kemp Harshman, Jose Heredia, Bill Hermann, Gary Heymann, Curtis Hoekstra, Eric Hovey, Neal Howard, Manny Otero, Joel-Steven, Michael Johnson, Lisa Kasberg, Rodger Kauffmann, Don Kilbury, Tim Knapton, Charles LaMantia, "Magic" Marc Lanning, Garrett LaPratt, Jack Lillian, Randy Lira, Mike Lonneman, Albert Lopez, David Louis, Ed Lovato, Bill Lovelace, Greg Lowder, Joe Martin (MO), Joe Martin (AZ), Joe Martin (TX), Matt Martindale, Jody & Tammy Maxx, Peter Merkle, Lisa Miller, Matt & Tamara Mitchell, Derrick Munoz, Wade Nelson, Jonathan Novich, Vicki Orgill, Cindy Ormond, Phil Peralta, Daniel Pizano, Robert & Stephanie Poff, Dodie Rahlmann, DJ Dr. Drax, Jim & Denise Sanchez, Steve Sharp, David Smith, Rob Snyder, Gil Sotelo, Randal Stout, Hugh Swanke, Jerry Taylor, Mark "Peace" Thomas and Susan, Scott Topper, Larry Williams, Shawn Willms, Scott Yoffe, Chris Allison, Joe Balice, Jeff Blugrind, Kelli Burns, Cap Capello, Jim Casey, Tom Catucci, John Christian, Chris Curto, Karl Detken, Brian Doyle, Richard Duffie, Andy Ebon, Aaron Fox, Tom French, John Gallagher, Scott Goennier, Ken Heath, Bob Holl, Jeff Hooten, Mark Hudnall, Craig Johnson, Jason Jones, Ron Jones, Brett Khan, Danette Koharchik, Greg "DJ Chopper" Lammers, Al Lampkin, Allen Layton, Dave Lewis, Brandon Lindsey, Nick Logan, Michael McCune, Scott McDonald, Bill James McElree, Alan & Debbie McKenzie, Chris Meschuck, Richard & Melanie Mills, Joseph Mire, Todd Mitchem, Stephen Moore, Calvin Morgan, Eric Moss, Derrick Munoz, Michael Peterson, Todd Powers, Kenny Quinterro, Toby Rechenamacher, Corey Rock, Orlando Rodriguez, Scott Siewert, Adam Skuba, Bill Smith, Terry Smith, Ty & Mari Smith, Xanthin Smith, Adam Sokool, Olyn Taylor, Mike Vaillencourt, David Van Enger, Timmy Vanderbilt, Mark Wakelin, Andrew Walker, Dude Walker, Dan Walsh, Robert Arthur, Cesar Cosio, Jeffrey Craig, Tom Daddazio, Bob Deyoe, Scott Faver, Tara Feely, "Sonny" Gallardo, Miles Gilbert, Jeffrey Greene, Joe Hecht, Johnny Kelly, Mark Klatskin, KC KoKoruz, Bob Kramarik, Marz & Amy Lawhorn, Jorge Lopez, Edwin McMurty, Ben Miller, Joe Murphy, Dan Ohrman, Mark Pedalino, Randi Rae, Rod Randall & Renee Retherford, Steve Roberts, John Rozz, J.R. Silva, Gerry Siracusa, Pete Troy, Mike Walter, Adam Weitz, Russ Welch, George Whitehouse, Bill Willets, Jared Bauman, Mike Colón, Chris Becker, Megan Gentile, Mike Gillmore, Julie Diebolt Price, Kevin & Renee Derek, Aaron & Jenn Delesie, Nicole Caldwell, Bob Stambach, Victor Sizemore, Dave Katinsky, Jack Randall, Jonathan West, Mandy Marie, Carl Young, Heather Howery and Rev. Clint Hufft.

On a personal note, special thanks are due to: My step-sons, Eric & Jason Lovato, my family in Seattle including: my brother Jesse, my sister-in-law Ramara, my nephew, Russell, my mother, Donna, my father, Pete, and the rest of the Merrys and Browns. This book is also dedicated to the memory of "my buddy" Carl Kudell. "Sweet!" will always be my favorite review.

And finally...I'd like to thank each and every couple who ever trusted me with their wedding entertainment. This book has only been made possible because you believed in me enough to keep me in business all this time.

foreword

What do people most often remember about a wedding? Surveys indicate that the most memorable moments occurred at the reception celebration following the wedding ceremony.

Now, that doesn't necessarily mean that the reception is remembered as a great event. Sadly, too often a wedding reception is long-remembered for all the wrong reasons.

In fairness, most engaged couples simply don't have the knowledge or experience that's required to organize an outstanding event. And that's precisely what a wedding reception is...an "event" that requires considerable thought and planning to transform it into a successfully entertaining celebration.

For the past 15 years, Peter Merry has helped hundreds of couples make the most of their wedding reception. He is an expert on what it takes to create a wedding reception that is fun, entertaining, and truly memorable (for all the right reasons). However, this is not just an opinion based on his credentials. I speak from first hand knowledge having been a guest at a reception where he was providing the entertainment. The next best thing to hiring him as your Wedding Entertainment Director™ is to use this ground breaking book as an indispensable guide that will help you to make the most of your wedding reception celebration.

So here's to your special day — may you and your guests hold cherished memories of your celebration as "The Best Wedding Reception...Ever!"

Tom Haibeck, Author
"Wedding Toasts Made Easy!" & "The Wedding MC"
WeddingToasts.com

introduction

As the guests arrive for the wedding reception, they can't help but notice how strikingly beautiful the ballroom looks. The floral centerpieces are mounted on golden stands displaying a vivid mixture of pink, lavender, green and red flower petals. The pale green linens on the tables give the room a feeling of being in an outdoor, garden setting. The favors feature a lavender ribbon tied in a bow on a small white box with the Bride and Groom's name and their wedding date in a handwritten font. The cake is set with four tiers and the frosting looks like a heavy, white ribbon that is rolling over the edges. The head table is on a riser with white lights illuminating the tablecloth from underneath the table. The appetizers are displayed with a touch of flair that clearly showcases the passion and creativity of the chef. The lights are slightly dimmed and the music playing in the background is a mixture of vocal jazz artists from the 40's and 50's singing songs about love. The catering staff begins to pour champagne as the MC tells the 200 guests in attendance that the Bride and Groom and their wedding party are almost ready to make their grand entrance.

Suddenly, the music volume goes up dramatically and the DJ begins to talk as if he's announcing the monster truck show on Sunday. The wedding party is introduced one couple at a time using just their first names. The Best Man is named John. He is the Groom's Father, but unless you were a friend of the Groom's family, you wouldn't have known that because the DJ fails to mention it. After the Best Man's toast, it's time for the Bride's Father and Stepfather to give a formal toast. The DJ takes the cordless microphone from the Best Man and walks to the center of the dance floor and introduces these two important men by saying, "Who wants it?", and then holds the microphone out at arm's length. Two men stand up and walk to the dance floor and make formal toasts, but unless you were a friend of the Bride's family, you wouldn't know their names, or which one of them was her Father or her Stepfather.

During dinner, the music is so loud that the guests have to shout in order to carry on a conversation. When the meal ends, the guests begin to get restless and it's a full 20 minutes from the time they have all finished eating until the special dances begin. The guests are overheard saying

"When does the fun begin?" The First Dance finally starts and when it ends, it's time for the Father/Daughter Dance. The DJ announces the Father/Daughter Dance and begins to play the specially selected song as the Bride stands on the dance floor waiting for her Father to join her. But he's nowhere to be found. "Where's Dad?" asks the DJ on the microphone. A few moments later, one of the guests runs out and locates the Father of the Bride in the restroom. When her Father finally makes it out to the dance floor, the DJ starts their song all over again after making a wisecrack at Dad for not being ready. When it's time to cut the cake, the MC invites the guests to gather around. But suddenly there's a commotion over near the cake as the photographer begins to make a frantic cutting motion with his hand and it becomes evident that there is no knife at the cake table. The Bride's Mother rushes over and tells a catering staff member, who disappears into the kitchen and then comes back with a knife so the Bride and Groom can finally cut their cake.

When everyone is invited to dance, the DJ tells the guests that they all have to come out to the dance floor if they want the Bride and Groom to have a long and happy marriage. He then guides them through a series of group dances as the Bride and Groom begin to shake their heads and it becomes obvious that these were songs that they neither liked nor had requested. There are many times throughout the remainder of the evening when the dance floor just remains empty. One by one the guests begin to bid the Bride and Groom farewell. Soon, more and more guests are leaving. They have the ballroom for another hour and when the reception is over, they share their Last Dance with 20 of their closest friends.

The day has ended, they are now married, they had a good time, and their reception was "okay."

As the Bride and Groom walk down the hallway on the way to their honeymoon suite, they pass a ballroom where another wedding reception has been going on at the same time as theirs. As they pass by, the doors swing open and they see 150 guests dancing, laughing, and enjoying themselves. They overhear a couple saying to each other as they leave the room, "That was the best wedding reception...ever!"

The Bride and Groom look at each other and begin to wonder what was so different about this reception compared to their own. "What did they do that we didn't?" they asked themselves.

The truth is there are many different styles of wedding receptions.

Some wedding receptions are ordinary while others are creative. Many Brides and Grooms want a traditional reception while others strive for a more contemporary feel. Wedding receptions can range from a boring routine to a crazy party. Some receptions seem to drag on forever while others seem to flow smoothly. At many receptions, the Bride and Groom are the central focus, while at others, guest involvement is encouraged. Some wedding receptions end hours earlier than planned, while others go the distance or are even extended for several additional hours so the celebration can continue.

This book is intended to give you the most current and creative ideas for making your wedding reception a true reflection of your personality and style. You will be given a wide variety of ideas. Some of these ideas may seem inappropriate for your plans, while others may leap off the page and connect with your innermost feelings about how you have envisioned your reception. Keep this in mind as you read on, because we all have different personalities, styles, and tastes. What works for you may not be right for somebody else. But when it comes to creating your wedding reception, there are no more rules. Follow your heart and choose the ideas that inspire you.

This book will also give you clear-cut examples of things that can go wrong, like the real life examples that were incorporated into the fictional story above, and will help you increase your chances of preventing them from occurring at your reception. Learning from the mistakes and oversights of others is an important step towards making your reception as flawless as possible.

To make the information in this book more accessible, it has been broken into three parts, which comprise the three major steps you will need to take in order to create a truly memorable wedding reception celebration:

Part I: Beginning Your Production—is all about choosing the right time, finding the perfect place, and selecting the best qualified cast of players to help make your reception fantastic.

Part II: Creating Your Timeline—is all about writing a reception plan that will flow smoothly so your guests won't ever feel bored or restless.

Part III: Adding Your Personal Style—is all about putting your fingerprints on every page of your reception plan so the music, guest interactions, and memorable moments will all feel like they were created uniquely for you.

Feel free to jump ahead to any chapter that features the information you are most interested in or the solutions to issues you are currently trying to resolve. Interspersed throughout this book will also be profiles of real couples and how their creative choices and ideas made their reception celebrations not only more fun, but also more memorable and personally meaningful as well.

You will find that this book does not contain ideas and suggestions related to the decorations, food, dresses, or ways to word your invitations. There are more than enough books available that have already covered those subjects in immense detail. But the ideas and suggestions that have not been presented in the ever-popular wedding planning books, or in the well-known wedding magazines, or even on the latest "reality" wedding television shows, are creative ideas directly related to ensuring that your guests will have a wonderful time, thanks to a well-paced atmosphere and personalized entertainment.

On that point, it is important to note that this book has been written from a unique perspective...one that is focused on the overall entertainment value of your reception.

"To capture and hold your guests' attention for an extended period of time."

This purpose statement sums up what most couples truly want their wedding receptions to do: capture and hold their guests' attention. They want their guests to stay for the whole party and enjoy themselves in the process. This purpose statement can also be condensed down to one simple word...entertainment.

The significance of this fact compels us to examine wedding receptions as more than just occasions for fancy decorations, beautiful flowers, elegant formalwear and pictures that will last a lifetime. Entertainment is the primary component that will make your wedding reception everything you've dreamed it would be. A wedding reception plan that fails to acknowledge the crucial role that the entertainment plays in keeping the guests involved, interested, and enjoying themselves, can quickly result in a wedding reception experience that is tedious and mundane.

Picture your Wedding Reception as if it is happening right now and think of the three primary words you would choose to describe what you see. Would you be surprised to know that the most common word that comes to mind is "FUN"? ("Elegant" and "Unique" rounded out the top 3.) If you truly want your guests to have fun at your reception, to feel like they are an important part of your celebration instead of just bystanders, then this book was written just for you.

However, this book is not intended to promote any particular style of entertainment. Many of the ideas contained in this book can be used with a Band, a Disc Jockey, a Wedding Entertainment Director™ or at a wedding reception that doesn't feature either. The key focus will be on recognizing simple methods that can make your reception truly fun, unique, and memorable—
because you deserve to have "The Best Wedding Reception...Ever!"

Also, for additional information on the subjects covered in the book, please feel free to visit these web sites:

TheBestWeddingReceptionEver.com
WeddingEntertainmentDirector.com
MerryWeddings.com
PeterMerry.com
WEDGuild.com

Enjoy!

THE
BEST WEDDING RECEPTION...EVER!
YOUR GUIDE TO CREATING AN UNFORGETTABLY FUN CELEBRATION

PART I

BEGINNING YOUR PRODUCTION
*Choosing the Right Time, Finding the Perfect Place,
and Selecting the Best Qualified Cast of Players*

Creating a fun, unique, and memorable wedding reception can be very similar to creating a blockbuster movie. Therefore, much of the terminology in this section will be purposely analogous to the arts and sciences of movie-making. Your wedding reception can (and will) be very entertaining, but there is a lot of foundational work that will need to be completed before we can properly set the stage for your opening night premiere. So let's get to work...

CHAPTER 1

DETERMINING THE TIMING
Choosing the Best Date, Day, and Time for Your Reception

Anyone will tell you that the date and time you choose for your wedding will have a major impact on the overall success of your day. Think about the movie industry—there's a good reason why blockbuster movies are released more commonly in the summer weeks. Kids are known for going to the same hit movie multiple times and so, because school is out, a summer release date can lead to greatly increased ticket sales. The movie's success can largely be a result of timing. In this chapter, we will explore the strategic advantages and disadvantages that need to be considered when selecting the date and time for your wedding reception.

The Saturday Evening Reception

It's pretty well known that a Saturday evening is the most popular day and time for a wedding reception. Here are a few of the benefits…

- ✚ Most of your guests will typically have the whole day off.
- ✚ Your guests will generally have the next day off as well, so they will be more open to staying out later.
- ✚ Saturday evening events tend to create a more elegant and relaxed atmosphere.

Here are some issues to consider when choosing a Saturday evening reception date:

Make sure that your ceremony is not starting too early, so that there won't be a huge gap of time between when your ceremony ends and your reception begins. Many local churches have restrictions on how late you can schedule to begin your ceremony on a Saturday. If your ceremony can't begin any later than 12:00pm, 2:00pm, or even 4:00pm, but your reception won't be able to begin until 5:00pm, 6:00pm, or even later…what will your guests do in the meantime? Some suggestions for preparing for this dilemma are given later in this chapter, in the section called "How to Bridge the Gap." It's probably obvious that scheduling your reception to begin directly after your ceremony is your best option.

Make sure the primary locations and vendors you want are available on your wedding date…before you set the date. Many of the best locations and vendors frequently book up their Saturday dates 9 months, 18 months, and sometimes even 24 months in advance, especially if the dates you are interested in fall into your area's wedding "peak season."

In Southern California, the wedding "peak season" often begins in April and typically doesn't slow down until well after October. In Phoenix, Arizona, weddings are rarely scheduled in the summer months due to the extremely high temperatures. Many areas around the country have varying peak seasons, so be sure to keep that in mind when determining your date.

In summary, here are some of the possible drawbacks to Saturday evening receptions …

- Possible lengthy gaps between the ceremony and the reception.
- Limited short-term availability of quality locations and vendors.
- Limited availability during your local area's "peak season" for weddings.
- Saturday evenings, being the most sought after time slots, will typically be booked at the highest rates by most wedding vendors.

The Saturday Afternoon Reception

Saturday afternoon receptions can also be an excellent option. Saturday afternoons share some of the same benefits as Saturday evenings, but there are some important differences to be considered. Here are some of the additional benefits…

- Lengthy gaps between the ceremony and the reception will no longer be an issue.
- Some locations and vendors may offer a "daytime" discount.
- Your guests can still enjoy a Saturday evening out on the town after your reception is over.

Here are some issues to consider when choosing a Saturday afternoon reception date:

You may not see as many guests dancing due to the "daylight factor." People generally feel more comfortable to let loose and "cut a rug" in an evening setting. There's something psychologically freeing about being in a darkened room when dancing is involved. Deep down, everybody is a little concerned that "if too many people can see me clearly when I'm dancing, they might think I look a little goofy." Good entertainment can compensate for this natural obstacle, and a location that has the ability to block or shut out the sunlight can help as well.

An afternoon time slot may limit the length of your event, as many locations are known for setting an afternoon time limit. It is very common for popular locations to require that afternoon receptions end by 4:00 or 5:00 pm, so that they can "turn" their room to prepare for an evening reception. This may have an impact on the overall entertainment of your reception, as your open dancing time may become limited as a result, especially if there have been any other delays (like the ceremony starting late or the photographs running longer than expected). If your guests are dancing and the party feels like it could go for an extra hour or two, some venues may not give you the option of extending your reception on a Saturday afternoon.

Because your reception will most likely be over before the evening sets in, some of your guests may be tempted to leave earlier than usual because they have made other plans for their Saturday evening. An early exodus can make a party feel like it's starting to wane, even if the majority of your guests are still dancing or enjoying themselves. But if you are mentally prepared for this to occur, it really won't have much impact on the overall enjoyment of your celebration.

In summary, here are some of the possible drawbacks to Saturday afternoon receptions…

- Daylight may impede your guests' desire to "boogie down" when it's time to dance.

- Your location may require that you end your reception on time or earlier than you might prefer.

- Any unforeseen delays could put an uncomfortable limit on the amount of time reserved for open dancing.

- Your guests may leave earlier than usual to prepare for their Saturday evening plans.

The Sunday Afternoon or Evening Reception

Sunday afternoon and evening receptions have basically the same benefits and drawbacks as Saturday afternoon and evening receptions, with two major additional benefits…

+ Some locations and vendors may be willing to offer substantial "Sunday Discounts" off of their regular pricing.

+ Availability of quality locations and vendors may be much better on Sunday afternoons.

However, Sunday evening receptions have one major drawback when compared to Sunday afternoon receptions (or Saturday afternoon and evening receptions). A majority of your guests will probably have to be ready for work on Monday morning, and therefore will be more inclined to leave earlier in the evening as a result. Sunday evening receptions can still be very entertaining, and there may very well be a good amount of open dancing. But if the reception starts too late or is scheduled to last until 11:00pm or later, you may find that a large number of guests leave earlier than desired. You can lessen this "mass exodus" effect by

---

RECEPTION DATE PROS & CONS

Saturday Evening
Pro: Relaxed Atmosphere
Con: Limited Availability

Saturday Afternoon
Pro: No Time Gap Issues
Con: Limited Overtime

Sunday Afternoon/Evening
Pro: More Availability
Con: Early Departures

Friday Evening
Pro: Friday Discounts
Con: Rush Hour Delays

Weekday Evening
Pro: Substantial Discounts
Con: Early Departures

planning for your reception to wrap up by 9:00pm or earlier. This will allow your guests to stay and celebrate with you longer, while still being able to get home in time to get some sleep before work the next day. If you are unable to schedule your reception to end by or before 9:00pm, the early departure of many guests may occur. But, once again, if you are mentally prepared for this to occur, it really won't have much impact on your overall enjoyment of your celebration.

In summary, the major possible drawback is…

- Your guests may be inclined to leave earlier than desired, as Monday is a common work day.

The Friday Evening Reception

Friday evening receptions have benefits and drawbacks similar to those of the options we have already examined. Here are some of the most common benefits…

+ Your guests will typically have the next day off, so they may be more open to staying out later.
+ Friday evening events can still create an elegant and relaxed atmosphere.
+ Some locations and vendors may be willing to offer substantial "Friday Discounts" off of their regular pricing.
+ Availability of quality locations and vendors may be much better on Friday evenings.

Here are some issues that may need to be considered when choosing a Friday evening reception:

Friday evening is the end of the work week and the end of a work day for many people. Most of your wedding party and some of your guests may need to take off the whole day from work in order to participate in or attend your wedding and reception. Some of your guests may need to take off a half day to be in attendance. Although most people would be glad to work a half day or take a day off, it may not always be convenient or possible for them to do so.

Friday evening rush hour traffic can lead to unexpected delays for you, your wedding party, and your guests. Being prepared for this contingency can alleviate any unneeded stress. One preventative option is to provide shuttle buses or a limo service to take care of your wedding party members' and/or your immediate family's transportation needs. The rush hour traffic may even cause delays amongst your vendors, so you might want to make sure that they intend to arrive earlier than normal.

After working a half day or even all day, some of your guests may feel a little worn out when it is finally time to open up the dance floor and cut loose. Instead of cutting a rug, some of them may choose to cut out earlier than you had expected because they may have already had a long day. But, as pointed out earlier, if you are mentally prepared for this to occur, it really won't have much impact on your overall enjoyment of your celebration.

In summary, here are some of the possible drawbacks…

- Your guests may need to take the day (or half the day) off from their jobs in order to attend.
- Friday evening rush hour traffic may cause unexpected delays for your wedding party, your guests, and even your vendors.
- Your guests may be inclined to leave earlier than you had desired, especially if they had to work a full or half day before attending your reception.

The Weekday Evening Reception

If you are considering a weekday evening reception, you will find a mixture of the benefits and drawbacks from the Friday evening reception and Sunday evening reception options. Here are some of the most common benefits…

- + Some locations and vendors may be willing to offer substantial "Weekday Discounts" off of their regular pricing.
- + Availability of quality locations and vendors may be much better on weekday evenings.

Here is a list of some of the possible drawbacks…

- Your guests may need to take the day off, or half the day off, from their jobs in order to attend.
- Weekday evening rush hour traffic may cause unexpected delays for your wedding party, your guests, and even your vendors.
- Your guests may be inclined to leave earlier than you desired, especially if they had to work a full or half day before attending your reception.
- Your guests may be inclined to leave earlier than you had desired as they will commonly have to work the next day.

The Impact of Holidays on a Reception Date

Holidays can provide an added benefit to particular days that might not otherwise have been as attractive. Here are some examples:

Memorial Day and Labor Day always occur on Mondays, thus enabling the Sunday evenings that precede them to share the same benefits that Saturday evenings normally have. The afternoons or evenings of Memorial Day and Labor Day can also be beneficial choices, as they will share the same benefits of a Sunday afternoon or evening reception. But these 3-day holiday weekends are also popular times for planning short trips, so you may need to send out your invitations a little earlier than normal, or at least send out "save the date" cards.

The 4th of July can create a 3-day weekend. This can allow a Thursday evening reception to share the same benefits as a Friday evening reception. On the same note, a Sunday evening reception can adopt the benefits of a Saturday evening reception. If the 4th of July occurs mid-week, the evening of July 3rd can have the same feel as a Friday evening reception. The 4th of July can also be a beneficial day for a wedding reception, especially if you are located near a large fireworks display and would like a patriotic theme. And of course, you can always joke with your friends that you picked that date as it will be a reliable way to make sure there are fireworks on your wedding night.

Thanksgiving always occurs on a Thursday and is generally a holiday that brings families together, even from long distances. Thanksgiving typically creates a 4-day weekend, which can give the Friday that follows it the same benefits of a typical Saturday. One added benefit of a "Thanksgiving Weekend" wedding reception is that you can save your extended family the expense of making another trip to come together at a different time for your wedding day.

New Year's Eve and New Year's Day offer their own advantages as well. Just like the 4th of July, New Year's Day can create a 3-day weekend or give a weekday added benefits. But the other advantage includes the state of mind that your guests are in when celebrating the New Year. They will not only be happy and ready to celebrate your new commitment to each other, but they'll also be in a party mood as the New Year approaches. However, some locations and vendors may not only have limited availability, but they may also require a premium fee for their location or services that may be a little higher (or even much higher) than their usual pricing. New Year's Eve is a popular night with a lot of demand, so don't be surprised if you need to exceed your budget expectations.

One drawback to consider in scheduling your reception around a holiday is that your friends and family may not wish to give up their entire holiday weekend to travel and attend your reception. If both of your families regularly congregate on various holidays, then this scheduling option might be a good fit. But if one or both of your families are known for heading out to a variety of destinations during a holiday weekend, then you might want to reconsider this option.

HOLIDAYS TO KEEP IN MIND

Memorial Day:
Last Monday in May

Labor Day:
First Monday in September

Independence Day:
July 4th (can create a 3-day weekend)

Thanksgiving Day:
Fourth Thursday in November (creates a 4-day weekend)

New Year's Eve & New Year's Day:
December 31st & January 1st (can create a 3-day weekend)

The Best Wedding Reception ...Ever!

The Impact of Large Sporting Events on a Reception Date

Large sporting events can also have an impact on the date you choose for your wedding reception. Here are some examples…

In 2002, the Southern California celebrations were impacted when the Los Angeles Lakers won their third straight NBA Championship and the Anaheim Angels also won the World Series for the very first time.

Game 7 of the Lakers semi-finals competition against the Sacramento Kings in 2002, was considered by many to have been the best game of the whole Championship series. There probably was no way that this could have been predicted when my clients had scheduled their wedding date, but this particular game drew more attention on that day than anything else in all of Southern California. During dinner, guests were congregating outside around small portable radios and televisions in an attempt to follow the game. Everyone could see them jump up and down when the Lakers took the lead and then moan and groan when the Kings moved ahead. I approached my clients with a few options for incorporating the situation, and they wisely opted to have me announce updates on the game throughout the meal, which I prompted by playing the theme from ESPN's Sports Center. By doing this, we kept a larger portion of the guests inside for the special dances, and when the Lakers finally won the game, it was just as we were beginning the open dancing. The guests' enthusiasm and energy was naturally exploding because of the Lakers crucial victory, and that energy spilled right over to the dance floor, which quickly raised the energy level of the dancing.

When the Anaheim Angels made it into the World Series for the first time in the history of their franchise, all of Orange County instantly became "die hard" baseball fans. I performed at three weddings that were impacted by the World Series. Two of them dealt with it smoothly, while one of them didn't fare quite as well.

The bride and groom of the two receptions that made positive use of the World Series games did what the couple in the previous example of the Lakers game did; they asked me to give regular updates of the score of the game… and when the news was good, I was more than happy to give those updates. In the reception that took a turn for the worst, the decline of the reception can be primarily attributed to the fact that my clients allowed a guest to bring in a small television, which was then set up and turned on so others could gather around and watch the game. Pretty soon, the guests were more focused on that little TV than on the real reason why they had come together to celebrate.

The point of this information is to show you that outside events can take a priority in the minds of your guests and, unless these circumstances are handled wisely, they can take over your reception in a detrimental way. So take some time to investigate whether any large sporting events (or other large scale events) might coincide with your prospective dates.

PROFESSIONAL SPORTING EVENTS

Pro Football
Playoffs
January
Super Bowl
Last Sunday in January or First Sunday in February

Pro Basketball
Playoffs
Mid-April through May
Finals
Early to Mid-June

Pro Baseball
Playoffs
Early to Mid-October
World Series
Late October

COLLEGE SPORTING EVENTS

College Football
Bowl Games
Mid-December to Early January

College Basketball
Final Four Playoffs
Mid-March to Early April

Determining
The
Timing

11

How to Bridge the Gap

If the gap between your ceremony and your reception is an hour or less, appetizers and appropriate background music should be more than enough to keep your guests entertained during the traditional "cocktail hour." But if your ceremony and reception are separated by a gap of more than an hour (or up to several hours), you should seriously consider bringing this issue to the attention of your invited guests. It is very helpful to find alternate activities for your guests to pursue while waiting for the proper time to arrive at your reception location. Listing some nearby points of interest, such as a theater, a museum, a historical site or even a mall, might go a long way towards helping your guests fill this "gap" of time between your ceremony and your reception. If the gap is unavoidable, proper preparation can at least help to alleviate the situation.

Suggested Reception Duration

One of the factors to consider when scheduling your wedding reception is determining how long your celebration should last. If you don't give yourself enough time, the time for dancing may get squeezed to a minimum and some of your reception events may begin to feel rushed. If you schedule too much time, your guests may leave earlier than you might have preferred, leaving you with just a small crowd at the end of the evening.

The best time frame for the duration of your reception is between 4 and 6 hours. Four hours is the minimum length of time I suggest to allot for your reception (ceremony not included), as it will give you just enough time to enjoy a meal, take care of all the traditional events you have scheduled, and still have enough time left for a good hour or more of open dancing. Six hours for a reception is a suggested maximum, as your guests will have been celebrating with you since your ceremony began. Keeping the party going too long will only be a problem if you are planning on having a big sendoff or if you want the majority of your guests to be involved all the way through to the end of your reception. If your reception plan includes dancing late into the night with a core group of your "party friends" (after most of the guests have already gone home), then preparing for a reception to last 6 hours or more might not be unreasonable. The longest weddings I have been involved with have lasted a total of 8 hours, including the ceremony and cocktail hour.

How Do You Want Your Reception to End?

The real question that needs to be examined when scheduling the length of your reception celebration is: what kind of an ending do you want your guests to remember? Comparing your wedding reception to a blockbuster movie, think back on how many movies you have seen that kept your attention and interest all the way through... but then ended poorly. No matter how good the rest of the film was, you will always remember it for having a weak ending. In the same way, your wedding reception can have a strong ending or an ending that trails off. Neither option is right or wrong. The only thing that matters is what kind of an ending will best fit your style. If your style is best reflected in a party that goes "all night long" with "the few, the proud, the party animals!", then by all means, schedule your reception to continue until midnight or later. But if your primary concern is that the majority of your guests can participate in seeing you off as you leave for your honeymoon, then you might want to prepare to end your reception at a high point, leaving your guests wanting just a little bit more. This type of ending can leave a positive lasting impact with your guests—one that you will be hearing about for years to come.

It is important to think in advance about the kind of ending you want, because when you are in the moment, you may feel inclined to "get your money's worth" from your location and/or your entertainment by going until 11:00pm as you had contracted, when a 10:00pm ending might result in a stronger and more memorable finale for your celebration. In the long run, if creating a memorable ending is your priority, then you will still get your money's worth by choosing to wrap things up at 10:00pm instead of 11:00pm, and your guests will still have an hour to say their goodbyes before the room has to be cleared.

Conclusion

There is a lot riding on the day and time you choose to have your wedding ceremony and reception. But above all else, be true to yourself when selecting the day and time for your wedding day. No matter what time or what day you choose, the all important focal point will be that the two of you will finally become Husband and Wife…and your friends and family will do their part to make it one of the happiest days of your life.

"What kind of an ending do you want your guests to remember?"

CHAPTER 2

MAPPING OUT A REALISTIC BUDGET
Examining Where to Spend and Where to Save

There once was a Father of the Bride who shared, during his toast at the reception, that when his daughter and wife had first approached him about preparing to finance the wedding day, he had told them both that they had an unlimited budget with which to develop their plans. He finished by pointing out that somehow they had managed to exceed that. How many times have you heard about a blockbuster movie going millions of dollars over budget? But then again, we've all seen blockbuster films that have failed miserably in the box office, while the small independent film that was created on a shoe string budget playing in the theater next door has brought in hundreds of millions in ticket sales. Having a large budget to work with isn't necessarily a guarantee of a quality entertainment experience for you and your guests. Most engaged couples today are either paying for their wedding themselves or are being assisted in some way by their immediate family. Mapping out a realistic budget will help you to determine many important factors that can have a direct impact on the style and type of wedding reception you can afford, as well as the number of guests you should consider inviting.

What are your priorities?

Establishing your priorities in advance will help you determine where your budget may need to be exceeded and where your budget may need to be trimmed. The big question that you will need to ask yourself is, "What facets of my wedding reception are most important to me?"

If you feel the photographs are most important to you, then you might want to set aside a larger portion of your budget for securing a photographer whose style and experience will be a perfect match for your desires. This priority will likely influence your choices of decorations, flowers, and apparel, so that your photos will truly look their best. But don't overlook the impact that the entertainment will have as well. The entertainment will help to create the fun, memorable moments that your photographer will be trying to capture.

If the most important component that comes to your mind is the food, (even though the food is already typically one of the largest expenses in a wedding reception budget), you will most likely select your location based on the type and quality of food that is served there. If you have less to spend on entertainment, your guests may not be inclined to linger

much past the end of the meal. But if the food is truly your biggest priority, then at least when your guests do choose to leave, they will leave having enjoyed a truly memorable meal.

However, if the most important component that comes to your mind is the entertainment, here are some facts you should consider before determining how much you can afford to invest in quality, personalized entertainment.

Some food for thought

If keeping your guests involved and appropriately entertained is of the highest priority to you, then you might want to ask yourself this question: "How big of a role will the quality of my entertainment play in the overall success of my reception?"

In post-reception surveys that were tabulated by DJs who are members of DiscJockeyAmerica.com, (an online forum where professional Mobile DJ's from around the world share ideas for creating better performances and improving their services), clients who made entertainment a high priority for their receptions answered the above question by stating that the quality of the entertainment they had secured was 80%[1] (or more) responsible for the success of their receptions.

For years, many have said, "the music makes or breaks the reception." But, the truth is that music is just one part of the overall services that professional wedding entertainment will commonly provide to ensure a great reception that is continuously entertaining for all of your guests. The statement would ring more true by saying "the *entertainment* makes or breaks the reception."

It's eye-opening to note that the popular wedding magazines, books, and TV shows will never give you advice on how to hire "film," because wedding photographers are already recognized as professionals and artists with unique talents, skills and personal styles. Yet those same bridal information resources are constantly offering tips on selecting "music" for your reception. Music is one of several elements that professional wedding entertainers will regularly provide. But if music were all that you needed to create an entertaining reception, the result would simply be an extended cocktail hour. The entertainment at a wedding (whether you choose a DJ or a Band) also typically serves as the Master of Ceremonies by announcing the formalities in an appropriate manner. The entertainment will help you plan the agenda to ensure the proper pacing needed to prevent your guests from becoming bored. The entertainment should communicate with you, your parents, your wedding party members, and your other vendors behind the scenes in an ongoing manner, keeping your reception agenda on track and flowing smoothly. The entertainment should also brainstorm with you to develop personalized moments that will leave your guests with lasting memories of your unforgettable celebration. Quality entertainment

The Best
Wedding
Reception
...Ever!

requires professionalism, artistry, and unique talent and skill, so don't be fooled into thinking that someone who will "just push play" on a CD player can make your reception fun and entertaining. . I will discuss these issues in greater detail in Chapter 7: "Auditioning for Talent."

In a survey that was featured in St. Louis Bride & Groom Magazine[2] in July of 2003, Brides who were surveyed within weeks of their wedding were asked, in retrospect, what they wished they had done differently when making their budget and hiring their vendors. 78% of them said they wished they had given top priority to their decisions about entertainment, and 72% of them wished they had spent more time researching before selecting their entertainment. That's a pretty high percentage of wedding clients who appear to be looking back at their recent entertainment decisions with buyer's remorse.

Nearly 100% of them said that, in retrospect, they would have gladly set aside more money from their budgets in an effort to secure a better quality of entertainment. This may be the result of the current budget suggestions in bridal magazines and popular bridal books that recommend setting aside only 5% to 10% of your total budget for the purpose of securing "music." But, as I mentioned earlier, music cannot create a successful reception all by itself. Overall, entertainment service is what really sets the tone, keeps the agenda flowing smoothly, and maintains the ongoing interest of the guests. Therefore it is my suggestion and conviction that investing more in the quality of entertainment that you desire for your reception is not a risk, but rather an investment in the overall success of your reception. How much is the success of your reception really worth? Is 15% of your total budget a fair amount? Is 20% of your total budget a fair amount? How about 25%? My goal in addressing these issues is not to convince you that a certain price range is correct or reasonable, but rather to expose you to this information in the hopes that your decisions in regards to your budget will be made with your most important priorities in mind.

In seminars and articles he has produced for the Mobile DJ industry, Mark Ferrell has repeatedly said, "The amount a person spends on entertainment is directly proportional to the quality of entertainment they will receive which is directly proportional to the overall success of their reception."[3] When movie producers want to make a successful comedy, they have been known to invest up to $25 million to secure Jim Carrey as the lead actor in the film. They are willing to spend this much because they recognize that Jim Carrey's track record and fan base ensures a film that will make at least $100 million, if not more, in return. How different is the entertainment you will select for your reception? Sure, your definition of a successful reception is much different than the definition of success for a blockbuster hit comedy movie, but the responsibility that Jim Carrey will have in helping to make the movie successful is very similar to the responsibility that your entertainment will carry in ensuring that your reception will be a success as well.

"Investing more in the quality of entertainment that you desire for your reception is not a risk, but rather an investment in the overall success of your reception."

If an entertaining reception is of the highest priority to you, keep in mind that there are many different aspects of your overall budget that may be easily trimmed without impacting the overall entertainment value of your reception in any way. I have seen wedding clients spend hundreds of dollars on favors (most of which get discarded), over a thousand dollars on chair covers, and tens of thousands of dollars on flowers. But when wedding guests have been polled in post-reception surveys about the most memorable aspects of the receptions they have attended, 80%[2] of them have said that the one thing they remembered the most was the entertainment. If you have attended any receptions lately, think back on them for a moment. Were they fun? Were they enjoyable? Were they entertaining, or were they boring? The most lavish of weddings can still be disappointing if the guests are bored or restless and the entertainment is not doing a good job of *entertaining*. On the other hand, a low-budget reception with less-than-incredible flowers, no chair covers or favors, and meager offerings for the meal, can still be an incredibly memorable reception if exceptional entertainment was a high priority.

A winning strategy

The top three aspects of a successful reception are the location, the photographer, and the entertainment. Finding a location that will fulfill your expectations, create great backdrops for your photos, and allow for a quality entertainment experience is crucial. Finding a photographer who can capture your memories with the style and quality you desire is vital. Finding entertainment that can work with your location and your photographer to create a smooth-flowing reception with memorable moments and personalized touches will be invaluable. As such, I would recommend that you do your research and select the best in all three categories that you can find. Then, survey the funds you have left in your total budget and begin working a strict budget from there. This strategy will give you a great foundation from which to build the "cast and crew" that will eventually make up the rest of your team of reception vendors.

Conclusion

$26,000 is the current average amount that is spent on a wedding day in the United States as reported on CNNmoney.com in May of 2005. A wedding day in New York City will easily average $30,000 or more, and a wedding day in Twin Falls, Idaho might average closer to $15,000 or less. Whether your budget is under $15,000 or upwards of $60,000 or more, your priorities will determine what you can and can't afford, and where you should or shouldn't be spending more than you had originally planned. Write a list of your priorities, and if hosting an entertaining reception is a high priority for you, then it is my hope that the information contained in the next few chapters will help you select the best vendors and get the best value for your budget.

PETE & NICHOLE
July 30th, 2005
Malibu, California

Let Them Eat...Double Doubles!

Pete & Nichole wanted to surprise their guests with something different for dinner. So, after the salads had been served, the guests were invited to guess what was going to be served for the entrée. Right on cue, the staff from In & Out Burger (a popular Southern California burger chain) came strolling out in their white uniforms with their red aprons and paper hats while the In & Out Burger jingle was playing. The guests began to cheer! Even though they saved a bundle on their food budget, you can clearly see that Pete & Nichole also got to enjoy their favorite meal on their wedding day.

*Father/Daughter-Mother/Son Dance

Pete & Nichole pre-recorded a special surprise message for her Father and his Mother which were then mixed into the Father/Daughter Dance and Mother/Son Dance songs.

RECEPTION AGENDA

5:50-6:50
Drinks & Appetizers
6:50
Grand Entrance
"You Really Got Me"
by Van Halen
7:00
First Dance
"Better Together"
by Jack Johnson
7:05
Toasts
7:15-8:15
Dinner
8:15
Father/Daughter Dance*
"Isn't She Lovely"
by Stevie Wonder
Mother/Son Dance*
"In My Life"
by The Beatles
8:25-10:00
Open Dancing
10:00
Cake Cutting
"When I'm Sixty-Four"
by The Beatles
"Satisfaction"
by The Rolling Stones
10:15-10:25
Bouquet & Garter Toss
"Naughty Girl"
by Beyoncé
"Hollaback Girl"
by Gwen Stefani
"Love Machine"
by The Miracles
"Lady"
by Lenny Kravitz
"Come Out And Play"
by The Offspring
10:25-12:30 (am)
Open Dancing
12:30 (am)
Last Dance
"It Ain't Over 'Til It's Over"
by Lenny Kravitz

PETE & NICHOLE

CHAPTER 3

PONDERING THE RESPONSIBILITIES OF A PRODUCER
Deciding Who Will be Your Lead Producer:
Do It Yourself, Enlist a Family Friend, or
Secure a Professional Coordinator?

Planning a wedding ceremony and/or reception can be a stress-filled task that may often feel chaotic and overwhelming. Trying to do it all by yourself can often lead to increased pressure, which may very well make you and those you are closest to feel miserable instead of ecstatic about your fast approaching wedding day. So how do you determine how much help you will really need? Is a professional coordinator always the best option? Could enlisting the services of a family friend be all you need, or would it be a sure fire recipe for disaster? Let's explore the responsibilities of a producer to help us better prepare for this decision.

What is the Role of a Producer?

A Producer in the movie industry has several important responsibilities. First and foremost, the Producer is the financial backer behind the movie. As the primary investor, the Producer has strong input concerning who will be the director, the lead actors, the set designers and the costume designers, and he or she also influences the locations for filming, the release date and, of course, the budget.

You and your immediate family (if they are helping to finance your wedding) are the Producers of your wedding day. Just as some independent films are produced on a shoe string budget by the director, who may also be the lead actor and screenwriter, a small scale wedding on a tight budget might be just fine as a "Do It Yourself" production. But when Hollywood wants to create a summer blockbuster with a budget of $100 million, they typically look for a tried and true Producer who has already produced some well known hit movies. In the same way, a professional coordinator who has already produced hundreds of successful weddings will not only help to relieve stress and anxiety, but they will also know the best options in locations, vendors, and decoration choices to fit within your budget and still fulfill your desires.

Keep in mind, however, that most Producers are not Directors. The role of the Director is to examine the script and rewrite certain scenes, if needed. The Director will inform the actors about how to best fulfill their roles: not only how to act as their characters, but also where they will need to stand and walk and sit for each and every shot. The Director will control the lighting and the pacing of the action. The Director will select the music that will create the best soundtrack for the film. The Producer and Director fulfill two very different roles. I will discuss these issues in greater detail in Chapter 8: "Nominating the Best Director."

The "Do It Yourself" Production

As I mentioned earlier, you are already the Producer of your wedding day. But, if you are planning on managing all of the Producer responsibilities by yourself, here are some things you might want to consider:

◆ Producing a wedding will take much longer than you might expect.

Most weddings take anywhere from nine months to a year or more to produce. Many weekends and weeknights will be sacrificed for location visits, vendor meetings, dress fittings, picking out rings, trying on tuxes, and selecting floral arrangements, not to mention bridal showers, engagement parties and bachelor/bachelorette parties. Examine how much of your own time you can afford to invest in your production. If you have the free time to manage these details, then a "Do It Yourself" production may be achievable.

◆ How much help will you really need?

Do you already have a pretty strong game plan, or are you at a loss for where to begin? Do you already have your location picked out, along with several of your key vendors? Do you have a clear idea of the type of decorations and flowers you will need and where to get them? Have you already found your dress and picked out the formalwear for your wedding party members? Then perhaps you can handle the other Producer details on your own as well. But, if you find yourself feeling overwhelmed after just leafing through a bridal magazine, then you might want to consider securing a professional coordinator.

◆ Who will manage the production details on your wedding day?

Who will make sure that your clothes are put where they need to be for your departure? Who will make sure that your gifts are properly secured or transported? Who will make sure the flowers from the ceremony are safely transported to your reception? Who will collect your guest book, your unity candles, your toasting glasses, your cake stands, and your cake knife? Who will make sure your place cards for the reception seating arrangements are put in their proper place? Who will look after your favors and make sure your centerpieces are set the way you wanted? If you already have a good answer prepared for all of these questions, then you might be prepared to pull off a "Do It Yourself" wedding reception. But, if you recognize that these details might have gone overlooked, then perhaps a professional coordinator will be your best choice. If you have most of the production details covered, but the details that need to be managed on your wedding day are still in need of resolving, then you might want to at least consider bringing on a "day of the wedding" coordinator.

Enlisting a Family Friend

When opting to enlist a family friend to serve as your wedding Producer, you may be working with a diamond in the rough or you may be taking a trip down a rocky road. Here are some issues to consider:

◆ How much wedding production experience do they have?

If they were recently married themselves, they may have some limited experience to share. If they have helped several other family friends to produce their weddings, how well did they do? Don't be afraid to ask for references or a portfolio of pictures and ideas if you have any reservations at all. If they are trying to start a wedding coordination service, will they be "learning from their mistakes" during your reception?

◆ You get what you pay for.

If they are managing your production responsibilities as a favor, will they revert to saying, "It's not like I'm being paid," if something goes wrong? To help alleviate any concerns for your big day, it is important to clearly define your expectations, as well as the roles and responsibilities of your Producer, in advance. If the Producer is being paid for his or her services, make sure it is a fair and reasonable amount for the services rendered. If he or she is serving as a volunteer, make arrangements to say thanks in a special way by arranging for a generous gratuity, a hotel suite for two, or something else that would be more meaningful on a personal level.

◆ Can your relationship withstand the pressure of wedding planning?

Is the person you are considering for a Producer someone you would feel comfortable saying "No" to? Would your relationship suffer harm if things went awry? Are you completely confident that the duties you will be entrusting to this person will be managed effectively? If there is any hesitation when approaching these issues, a professional coordinator may be a better option for the sake of your current relationship with this family friend. Better to retain your friendship with this person and maintain your own sanity, than to lose both in the tumultuous events that can unfold during the chaotic process of wedding production.

The Professional Wedding Coordinator

If you recognize that you will need a true professional to help you with the production of your wedding day, selecting the right person will have a dramatic impact on the overall success of your reception. A professional wedding coordinator will help turn your visions into reality while also helping you to select vendors that will make up your winning team. However, finding the right person for the job can be a challenge. Here are some things to consider:

"Are you completely confident that the duties you will be entrusting to this person will be managed effectively?"

◆ How much wedding production experience do they have?

A professional wedding coordinator should have a portfolio of client references, unique wedding ideas, and preferred vendors. Do your research, call their references, and talk to the vendors they recommend. Keep in mind that some wedding professionals may have many years of experience, but tend to merely do the same exact kind of weddings over and over again for years. Look for diversity in the type and style of weddings that they have produced.

◆ Is this a person I can work with?

There are different types of services provided by wedding coordinators. Some will manage all of the details while seeking your input on all of the available options. Others will give you a few choices while making many of the style choices themselves. Neither approach is right or wrong. They just cater to different types of clients. How little or how much of the detail work you want to be involved with is up to you, but once you have determined how involved you want to be, then the type of coordinator who will best fit your needs should become apparent. Remember, this is a person you will be working with very closely over several months. Finding a personality match should also be an important part of the decision.

◆ Will your coordinator work as a team player with your other vendors?

A team player is a person who recognizes that constant and mutually respectful communication is an important ingredient in accomplishing a successful wedding reception. How soon will your coordinator make contact with your other vendors? Will it be the week of the wedding, or right after they have been hired? Advance contact from the coordinator gives your other vendors the confidence that your production details are in good hands. A coordinator who waits until the week of the wedding to make first contact with your other vendors will result in unneeded stress and anxiety for your vendors and for you, as they may have questions and issues that are hard to answer or resolve with less than a week to go.

What about at the wedding reception? What if the coordinator is not getting along with your photographer? Will their issues be resolved professionally? Ask your coordinator about challenges they have faced with other vendors and what they did to resolve them. Professional coordinators have worked with some of the best and some of the worst wedding vendors around, and they have undoubtedly encountered tense and trying situations with some of them. Pay close attention to the coordinator's answers and look for strategies they have developed as a result of these situations for preventing them from occurring in the future. If no strategies have been developed, then they may be placing the blame elsewhere instead of actively seeking solutions.

"The duties of a Producer cannot be overlooked when creating an entertaining reception."

◆ What preparations has your coordinator made for emergencies?

A professional coordinator is prepared for just about everything. They commonly carry an emergency kit filled with buttons, needles, thread, candles, lighters, matches, shoe polish, make-up, antacids, and other items that in the heat of the moment can turn a near-disaster into a heroic save. Professionals are prepared. Ask your coordinator about the preparations they have made to prevent problems (or to resolve them, should they occur). Ask to see a checklist of the details that the coordinator will be managing to prevent those details from being overlooked. Ask about their emergency kit, or about the last fiasco (or near fiasco) that they encountered and how it was effectively resolved.

◆ Will your coordinator allow the entertainment to give input regarding the reception agenda?

A professional coordinator will value the input provided by your entertainment regarding the room layout, the reception agenda, and the music selections. Part of the professional coordinator's role is to help you choose the best vendors—vendors whose expertise you will rely on to help you create the kind of reception you've been planning. If the coordinator is unwilling to meet with or work with your entertainment vendors in advance, then you might be allowing a Producer, who possibly has little or no entertainment experience, to create an agenda that might not be very entertaining. Your coordinator will trust the florist to give input on the floral arrangements and they should be just as open to creative input from your entertainment vendors.

◆ What is your coordinator's policy regarding a preferred vendors list?

Professional coordinators will refer and recommend the best quality vendors they can find within your budget range because they recognize that truly professional vendors make them look even more professional in return. However, some coordinators may make a referral based on a referral fee they receive from vendors for securing their services. This practice, although somewhat common, may not be serving your best interests. If your coordinator limits your vendor options to vendors who provide them with additional income on the side, these vendors may or may not be the best quality vendors for your needs. This apparent conflict of interests may not matter to you, but if it does, don't be afraid to ask pointed questions about this before selecting your coordinator.

Conclusion

Whether you opt to go for the "Do It Yourself" wedding reception production, enlist a family friend, or secure the services of a professional wedding coordinator, keep in mind that you are still your own lead Producer—this is your production. Whether you choose to delegate these responsibilities to a hired professional or not, the duties of a Producer cannot be overlooked when creating an entertaining reception.

CHAPTER 4

SCOUTING FOR THE PERFECT LOCATION
Finding the Right Venue for Your Ceremony and/or Reception

Selecting the right location can be very complicated as the place you choose to get married and/or celebrate your day will set the stage for your complete reception experience. Finding a venue that will match your style and deliver the level of service you require is similar to finding the right environment for filming a scene in a movie that needs to occur in a desert or in a tropical paradise. If the wrong location is selected for the film shoot, the backdrop and setting won't match the context of the film. I'm sure you've seen countless films where the characters were supposed to be driving through the outskirts of Seattle or in the countryside of England...but in reality it was obvious that they were really driving through the hillsides of Southern California. In the same way, choosing the wrong venue can cause similar problems in the overall continuity of your wedding reception plans.

Ceremony Sites

Choosing the ceremony site that will be perfect for your plans requires examining several different factors. If you and/or your fiancé had a religious upbringing, then getting married in a church or a synagogue might be your first choice. Many wedding ceremonies also occur in alternative locations such as: country clubs, banquet facilities, public parks, and private homes. Each type of ceremony site has its own set of benefits and drawbacks, but here some general questions to ask for starters.

◆ How far away is my ceremony site from my reception location?

Too much distance between your Ceremony and Reception locations can result in guests attending the Ceremony but skipping out on your Reception or getting lost or stuck in traffic on the way to your Reception.

◆ What is the earliest time we could schedule our ceremony to begin?
◆ What is the latest time we could schedule our ceremony to finish?

These two questions are crucial to ask in advance for several reasons. Some churches and ceremony locations do multiple ceremonies per day or they may have services in the later afternoon or early evening. Being aware in advance about your time constraints may be helpful in choosing a ceremony site. Awareness of these possible constraints can also equip you to make a solid game plan to use your time at the location

effectively. As detailed in the previous chapter, if your Ceremony site can only be available until 3:00pm, but your Reception location will not be available until 6:00pm, this may have a negative impact on the length of your Reception celebration later.

◆ Is there enough room for all of my guests to be seated comfortably?

Some Ceremony sites only have room for limited seating, leaving the majority of your guests to stand during your Ceremony. Are you willing to sacrifice your guests' comfort for a unique location that might result in some remarkable ceremony photos? Either way, you are better off knowing before the location is secured.

◆ Is there enough parking for all of my guests?

If not, you may want to consider hiring a valet service so your guests aren't late due to hunting for parking spots off the beaten path at the last minute.

◆ Is there electrical power available for the musicians and/or DJ?

Some Ceremony sites, like public parks, feature no power supply at all. A quiet generator may be required for amplified PA support and music. Some Ceremony sites have power, but at a considerable distance from where the musicians and/or DJ may be setting up. Knowing how much extension cord for power will be required can prevent any mishaps on the big day.

◆ Is there any history of radio interference with wireless microphones in the area?

Some Ceremony sites have a well-documented history of radio interference that can interrupt the Minister's cordless lavaliere/lapel microphone during the Ceremony. Especially if the Ceremony site is close to the ocean or a military base featuring an abundance of radio interference. Your PA support will need to be adjusted if such a history exists at your Ceremony site.

◆ Is there any nearby traffic that could add unwanted noise during my Ceremony?

One beautiful location in Southern California has a Ceremony site that is right up against a back-roads highway that is well known for Harley Davidson biker traffic. The sound of throbbing Harley engines cruising by is a common "addition" to the Ceremonies I have been involved with at this particular location. Become familiar with the surrounding of your Ceremony site to be aware of these types of unexpected noise issues. Sometimes the setting is stunning enough on its own that a little traffic noise is an easy sacrifice to make.

◆ What is the availability for scheduling the Wedding Ceremony Rehearsal?

Some Ceremony sites will not be able to accommodate a Friday night Rehearsal for a Saturday Reception due to the frequent capacity for booking Friday evening Weddings or other events. Thursday evening or Friday afternoon may be your only options as a result.

◆ Does the location provide a ceremony coordinator, or will we need to provide our own?

Some locations will require that you use their on-staff coordinators, while others will require you to provide your own qualified coordinator as a pre-requisite for using their location. Keep in mind that some on-staff coordinators may have their location's preferences and agenda prioritized higher than your own.

◆ Will the location's coordinator work as a team with my other vendors?

Interview other vendors who have a history of working with the location's on-staff coordinator to find out if you are getting a qualified team player. Be sure to meet the on-staff coordinator in person so you can be confident and comfortable with the person you will be working with on your wedding day. One couple I worked with closely in September of 2003 were caught completely off guard at their Rehearsal when they were introduced for the first time to the on-site coordinator who had been selected to "handle" their ceremony and reception. Having never met with or been told that this person would be their primary contact for the location for their wedding day, their confidence levels began to drop rapidly. Clearly defining who they would be actually working with in advance would have prevented a large amount of unneeded stress so close to their big day.

◆ Will the location's coordinator allow me to create my own ceremony schedule?

Some locations have their own ideas about how your Ceremony should occur. Be sure to find this out before you choose your location. If they use phrases like "We usually like to…" or "This is the way it's done here." then you may be walking into a location that could hijack your Ceremony plans with their own agenda or traditions. It's your Wedding Ceremony and you deserve to have the kind of Ceremony you've always wanted.

◆ Will the location's coordinator direct my Ceremony Rehearsal?

Some location coordinators will commonly and confidently guide and direct your Ceremony Rehearsal for you, while others may prefer to serve primarily as your liaison with the catering staff. Be sure to clearly

"It's your Wedding Ceremony and you deserve to have the kind of Ceremony you've always wanted."

define who will be assuming this important role and make sure that this person is willing to do some advanced planning with you well before the Rehearsal. Rehearsals are for your wedding party members and immediate family to rehearse your wedding ceremony. They shouldn't have to stand around waiting because the appropriate planning was not already done in advance. Also, someone who is less-than-informed about your details can create more stress or lead to embarrassing moments. One location coordinator I observed who was directing a rehearsal without the appropriate amount of advanced planning, began telling the Bride's Father that he was not supposed to be sitting on the aisle seat because that seat is traditionally reserved for the Mother of the Bride. She then began asking where the Bride's Mother was, to which that Bride pointed out that her Mother had been deceased for many years. Choose the person who will direct your Rehearsal wisely. Their role is important and should not be overlooked.

Reception Locations

Choosing the Reception location that will fit your needs and fulfill your vision can be a daunting task. Some locations may be too big while others may be too small. Some locations my look beautiful and yet have horrible acoustics. Some locations can offer you the world while others may feel like they are maintained by beings from another planet. Here are some helpful questions that may guide you in selecting the location that is just right for your Wedding Reception.

◆ What are the time restrictions for the location?

Some locations can do multiple events per day and may require you to fit into their schedule. You may have to choose between a 12:00noon to 4:00pm time slot or a 6:00pm to 10:00pm time slot. Other locations may only do one event per day, thus allowing far more flexibility in your start and finish times. Some locations may have a 4 hour maximum while others may offer unlimited time. Some locations may prefer a 4 or 5 hour block of time to start, with an option to extend your celebration for an additional fee.

◆ How early can my vendors arrive to begin setting up and decorating?

Most locations will allow 90 minutes as a minimum with up to 2 or 3 hours of lead time for your vendors to begin setting up and decorating. Some locations, however, may only allow 1 hour or even only 30 minutes for your vendors to get their decorations in place or to set up and test out sound equipment. This may be too constraining for some of your vendors. The location may say they provide an hour of set up time, but if they have an earlier function in the room that ends one hour before your reception is scheduled to begin, your vendors will be lucky if they are provided even 30 minutes to get completely set up. This can make your other vendors appear to be running late, when actually the situation has been entirely beyond their control.

◆ How late can my Reception last before we have to close down?

Some locations have noise restrictions after 10:00pm. Find out what your location's restrictions may be in advance before deciding what time to begin your reception. If you want the option to have your reception last until Midnight or later, this bit of information will play a crucial role in finding the right location to suit your needs.

◆ Will all of my guests fit comfortably in the same room?

Some locations may only be able to fit a limited number of your guests in the main room, while requiring the rest of your guests to be placed in an overflow room or patio. This can cause some of your guests to feel disconnected from the celebration, especially if the entertainment isn't prepared to provide the needed PA support to the overflow area. On the other side of the coin, if the room is too large, your guests may feel too spread out and it may be more difficult to get them involved when it's time to dance.

◆ How close is the Reception location to the majority of my guests' homes?

If the majority of your reception guests are traveling over 30 minutes just to attend your reception, they may be inclined to leave earlier than you'd like because they have a long drive ahead of them. One Sunday evening Reception I performed at years ago was at a hotel in Laguna Beach, but the majority of the guests were from Pasadena, which is over an hour drive away. Even though they had scheduled the Reception to last until 10:00pm, most of the guests began to leave between 8:00pm and 8:30pm because many of them had to work the next day and they still had over an hour worth of driving to do before they would even arrive home. If the majority of your guests are flying in and are staying at a nearby hotel, this might not be too big of a concern for you as they may be more inclined to stay later.

◆ If the Reception location is outdoors, what are the precautions for bad weather?

Some locations may have a tent and space heaters prepared as a back-up for inclement weather while others may need to move the celebration indoors. If a back-up plan is not already in place, bad weather could put a damper on your day and your budget. On the flip side, if your location is outdoors and the weather is bright and sunny with sweltering heat, a lack of table umbrellas may leave your guests soaking in sweat well before the dancing even begins.

◆ If the Reception is indoors, are the environmental controls reliable?

A room without heat on a cold winter night or a room with no air conditioning on a hot summer afternoon can both make for a reception

that is unbearable for your guests. Be sure to check with your reception location to ensure that they have appropriate and reliable environmental control systems in place.

◆ What are the options for controlling the natural and electric lighting?

If your Reception is during the day, and your location has large bay windows that cannot be covered with drapes or shades, your guests will be dancing in the daylight. A brightly lit room and exuberant dancing are usually not a good combination, although a qualified entertainer can still render a good response. But, if the room has the capacity to draw shades to block out some of the daylight, a matinee effect will create the illusion of an evening reception in the mid-afternoon which will in turn create a better atmosphere for dancing. If your reception location has only fluorescent lighting and no dimmer switches, creating the right atmosphere for your reception may be a bit of a challenge. Test out the lighting at your location and see which settings are available. See if the room lights can be set to an appropriate level for dinner and maybe even a darker setting for dancing at the end of the evening.

◆ Will they allow your entertainment to set up next to the dance floor?

Believe it or not, some locations actually require your entertainment to set up in a back corner or on a remote stage with tables of guests who are then unfortunately located between the speakers and the dance floor. This not only prevents the dance floor from attaining the appropriate volume levels for enthusiastic dancing, but it also forces the guests at these unlucky tables to suffer extremely high volume levels throughout the reception. Be sure to ask where your entertainment will be required to set up in relation to the dance floor at your location of choice.

◆ Does the room layout allow for a centrally located dance floor?

Upon viewing a country club for an upcoming reception, I was informed by the location's catering manager that the dance floor was usually set up at one end or the other of this basic rectangular room. When I asked if they had ever set up the dance floor in the center of the room, the catering manager said, "Oh no, that would just leave a big hole in the middle of the room." What she saw as a "big hole" was in reality "center stage" for most of the traditional wedding reception events. If your dance floor is at one end of a long room, in separate room from the guests or around a corner, your guests may feel left out when it is time for your First Dance or the Bouquet Toss. A centrally located dance floor is easy to access for dancing, is more accessible for guests who want to watch the traditional events, is convenient for the catering staff as a place for staging the trays of food they will be serving and will go a long way towards making everyone feel more involved in your celebration. If the location you are considering does not already offer a centrally located dance floor, ask them if they are willing to try such a layout for your reception. The following room layout diagrams might be helpful:

These are examples of room layouts that can be problematic:

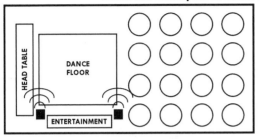

These are examples of room layouts that would be considered optimal:

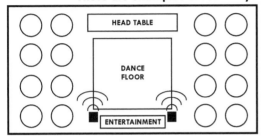

◆ Is there any history of radio interference with wireless microphones in the area?

Some Reception locations have a well-documented history of radio interference that can interfere with the cordless microphone during the formal Toasts. If the location is close to the ocean or a military base featuring an abundance of radio interference, you may want to inform your entertainment provider.

◆ If we choose buffet service, will the number of buffet lines be increased to accommodate for a larger guest count?

If you have one buffet line for over 200 guests, be prepared for the buffet service to last well over an hour. As your guests count grow, locations that are prepared to handle the increased number of guests will typically add additional buffet lines to allow more guests to be served in a shorter period of time. A buffet dinner that drags on unnecessarily long can put a damper on the overall mood of your reception.

◆ Does the location provide a reception coordinator, or will we need to provide our own?

As with your ceremony needs, some locations will require that you use their on-staff coordinators, while others will require you to provide your own qualified coordinator as a pre-requisite for using their location. As with your ceremony needs, some on-staff location coordinators may have their location's preferences and agenda prioritized higher than your own.

Scouting
For The
Perfect
Location

♦ Will the location's coordinator allow me to create my own Reception schedule?

As mentioned earlier, some locations have their own ideas about how your reception agenda should flow. It is vital that you find this out in advance. If their preferences have been set up to facilitate their needs, the food may be served just the way they like it, but the reception may lack the steady flow that will keep your guests thoroughly entertained. One such location had a policy of requiring the Bride and Groom to cut their cake right after the Grand Entrance and the Toasts so they could serve it as dessert and then send some of their catering staff home, thus saving on payroll costs. Although this idea by itself is not necessarily wrong, the purpose behind it combined with it being a requirement for that location prevents couples who select that location from considering other options for their reception agenda that might be more in line with their own preferences and style. Don't let your location dictate your reception timeline if it clashes with your own ideas, after all, this is your wedding reception, not theirs.

♦ How many events will be occurring at the location during your reception?

Some locations may commonly host more than one reception per day. In some rare occasions, certain locations may even host upwards of four or more ceremonies and/or receptions on the same premises. Not only could this lead to possible confusion for your guests and/or vendors, but it could put a damper on your celebration of the other ceremonies are located too closely to your reception location.

In April of 2002, I had the unique opportunity to participate in a wedding ceremony and reception at a location can that best be described as a wedding factory. My clients were holding their ceremony at the location's gazebo which was a mere 80 feet from the open courtyard where their reception was to be hosted. This courtyard was surrounded by a four foot high hedgerow, and we were notified by the location just three days before the wedding that they had two more ceremonies scheduled to occur at the gazebo during the time we would celebrating my client's reception. Because our reception was set to occur so close to those additional ceremonies, the location told us we would have to turn down the music during both ceremonies. Needless to say, this was not only disconcerting and distressing for my clients, but it was also rather daunting news for me as well. After weighing our options, I advised my clients that we could schedule certain parts of their reception agenda to allow for the music to be turned down without causing too much negative impact on the entertainment value of their reception. Because we knew when the next two ceremonies were scheduled to begin, we adjusted the timing for the beginning of the meal to coincide perfectly with the start of the first ceremony. Having the background music play lower than normal during dinner was a great solution. We had also adjusted our agenda for the second ceremony, and as my clients had

The Best
Wedding
Reception
...Ever!

opted to do a Money Dance, I suggested we should try to start the money dance just before the next ceremony so the volume being lowered would once again fit the moment and not cause guests to get bored or restless. Our timing was perfect and we started the money dance right on schedule, but the second ceremony didn't get started for another 15 minutes. Needless to say, our Money Dance ended before the second ceremony was over and the low volume we were required to maintain was not conducive for a dancing atmosphere. As a result, their reception ended earlier than we all would have liked, and my clients were very upset with the location's management.

◆ What is the location's policy regarding their preferred vendors list?

Most locations have a list of preferred vendors whom they are happy to recommend. Some locations give these recommendations based on professionalism and quality of service that they have personally witnessed repeatedly. These locations recognize that professional vendors who provide a quality service in a reliable manner not only do right by their clients, but they also make the location look good in return. Other locations, however, will refer vendors who offer them a finder's fee or are willing to put the location's agenda preferences above those of their clients. In these cases, the location's reasons for referring the vendors that they do may not have your best interests in mind. In some rare occasions, the location may actually attach an additional "damage deposit" or penalty fee for using vendors who are not on their preferred vendor list. Read the fine print before signing to secure such a location. These added fees are designed to "encourage" you to choose their preferred vendors, who may not be either the best qualified or the right vendor for your needs. It's your wedding reception and it is only going to happen once. Don't let anyone force you to choose vendors that you are not completely comfortable hiring.

Conclusion

Finding the right location and securing your date will become the cornerstone for guiding all of the other decisions you will make. Your location will influence your decisions about flowers and decorations. It may influence the type of photographer you choose. It will directly impact the environment that is created during your reception. Don't compromise or settle for less. Choose the location that not only fits your style, but will also help facilitate a better entertainment experience for you and your guests.

"Choose the location that not only fits your style, but will also help facilitate a better entertainment experience for you and your guests."

CHAPTER 5

SELECTING THE SET DESIGNERS
Thinking About the Flowers, Décor, and Lighting

The set design on a movie helps to create the theme and environment that the audience is expected to accept as reality. If the sets are built in such a way that the main characters are blocked from view in most of the shots, the patrons may leave the theater early because they can't follow the plot. As we examine the issues to consider regarding the decorations for your reception, please keep in mind that there are many books already written that can advise you in vast detail about style, fabrics, design, and décor. However, there are some important entertainment issues that should be considered when preparing to decorate for your wedding reception.

Overgrown Centerpieces

One of the most common mistakes made when designing reception decorations is choosing centerpieces that are too large and block the clear line of sight that serves to increase your guest's feelings of involvement. If your guests can't clearly see the person seated across the table from them, not only will table conversations be impeded, but many of them will not be able to clearly see the grand entrance, the formal toasts, or maybe even your First Dance. The more disconnected your guests feel, the more likely they will be to leave early. This problem can easily be resolved by choosing smaller centerpieces, or by putting the larger centerpiece, on a tall, narrow stand thus opening the sight lines throughout the room.

Room to Jump Around

Another common decorating mistake is using low-hanging décor over the dance floor. Decorative tulle twisted with twinkle lights can create a nice look, but if it is hanging too low over the dance floor, it can be easily damaged when the dancing gets underway. At a wedding in November of 2005, the tulle and twinkle lights were hung so low over the dance floor most people had to duck just to walk under it. When the dancing was in full swing, a groomsman, who had drank more than his share of alcohol, began pulling on the tulle and eventually pulled a good portion of it down while he was dancing. This inconvenience not only created a hazard for people walking by, but it also ruined the ambiance these decorations had been creating. If they had been draped higher up, they would not have been so easy (or tempting) to rip down.

Burning Up

Flammable decorations and votive candles can be both beautiful and dangerous at the same time. If you choose to use votive candles for decorative purposes, be sure to put them in containers that are taller then the candle's flame. If the containers are too low and the candle's flame is exposed, there will an increased risk that a napkin or centerpiece decoration could catch fire. I personally witnessed a female wedding guest whose sleeve on her polyester outfit came too close to an open flame on a votive candle and caught fire. Polyester combusts very quickly and in less than a second her whole top began to catch fire. Luckily the photographer quickly smothered this guest and put out the flames. Everyone was shocked by what they saw, and the female guest was taken to the hospital.

Fire is not a laughing matter. Check with your location on their restrictions regarding candles and open flames before making any final decisions. Also, some candles put off smoke, so if you want to use colorful, creatively shaped candles, give them a test burn to see if they give off light emissions or heavy smoke before you commit to using them at your reception.

Shedding a Little Light

If the location offers colored up-lighting to change the ambience of the room, these up-lights should be on dimmer switches so the brightness can be adjusted as the dancing begins. Providing spotlights for the grand entrance, the toasts and the special dances may also be necessary. In August of 2005, one of my clients opted for an up-lighting package that added nice coloring to the room and even put spotlights on the centerpieces for each table. But the room's normal lighting had to be dramatically reduced so the up-lighting and spotlights would have desired impact. However, there was no provision made for properly lighting the grand entrance or the toasts, and so, as the wedding party entered and the toasts were taking place, the guests could barely see what was happening. Later in the evening, when the dancing was underway, the up-lighting and spotlighting was too bright and needed to be dimmed down, but none of the lights were on dimmer switches and the energy on the dance floor may have been negatively affected as a result.

Conclusion

The right decorations will give your reception a look that should create a memorable impression. But decorations that are too large, poorly placed, or dangerous can create the wrong kind of memories for your guests. Be safe, be creative, and have fun. Let your decorations dress your set and enhance the environment for your celebration.

EVAN & CHRISTINE
July 15th, 2005
Solvang, California

Chinese Lanterns Under the Stars

Evan & Christine celebrated their Reception on his parent's ranch in Solvang. Just a year earlier, when we were meeting to discuss their plans for the first time, we all took a walk down into the dry gully next to Evan's parent's home to survey their proposed location. It took some imagination then, but with a little grading, a fresh layer of green grass, and some Chinese Lanterns draped overhead, the dry gully was transformed into a fantastic setting for a memorable party.

*"NFL Theme"

Evan & Christine first met while going to school at Cal Poly San Luis Obispo. To make their Garter Toss more fun, they both autographed a CPSLO Mustangs football. Then Evan wrapped the Garter around the football before tossing it into the air so the single guys could all scramble for it.

RECEPTION AGENDA

6:00-7:20
Drinks & Appetizers
7:20
Grand Entrance
"Celebration"
by Kool & The Gang
7:30-8:40
Toasts & Dinner
8:40-9:00
The Special Dances
First Dance
"Sea Breeze"
by Tyrone Wells
Father/Daughter Dance
"Because You Loved Me"
by Celine Dion
Mother/Son Dance
"I Hope You Dance"
by Lee Ann Womack
Parents & Wedding Party
"The Way You Look Tonight"
by Frank Sinatra
9:00-9:30
Open Dancing
9:30
Cake Cutting
"Grow Old With You"
by Adam Sandler
"Ice Cream"
by Sarah McLachlan
9:40
Bouquet Toss
"Girls Just Want To Have Fun"
by Cyndi Lauper
"You Sexy Thing"
by Hot Chocolate
9:45
Garter Removal & Toss
"Bad Boys (Cops Theme)"
by Inner Circle
"Mission: Impossible Theme"
by Larry Mullen & Adam Clayton
"NFL Theme"*
from Fox Sports
9:50-11:15
Open Dancing
11:15
Last Dance
"Good Riddance"
by Green Day

EVAN & CHRISTINE

39

CHAPTER 6

SCREENING THE CINEMATOGRAPHERS
Evaluating Your Photographer and Videographer

When a movie director yells, "Cut! That's a wrap!", it usually means that the principle photography has been finished for the day. But we are all familiar with the terms, "Take 2...Take 3," which are used when an actor is asked to re-do a scene several times until the director feels the right moment has been captured. However, on your wedding day, there are some special moments that will need to be captured for which there will be no opportunity for a "Take 2." The moments you want captured on film and how you want them to turn out are choices that are extremely personal. Finding the right photographer to capture those moments in a style that matches your desires can be downright challenging. Choosing a videographer who can document one of the happiest days of your life and then deliver an edited final product that is enjoyable to watch may feel daunting. But there are also a few important considerations from the entertainment perspective that should be examined. This chapter will attempt to bring those issues into sharp focus.

Shutter Drag

One of the most common ways that the photographer you choose can impact the success of your reception is related to timeliness. Most wedding photographers can finish up with your post-ceremony family, wedding party and romantic shots in 45 minutes to an hour. But if the photographer you select takes 2 hours, and your guests are left waiting along with the chef, the party atmosphere at your reception can take a dive very quickly. Feel free to ask your photographer about their time requirements and be sure to ask their references how timely they actually were on the wedding day. At a recent reception, the photographer told me he would be taking the bride and groom out for some "quick" sunset photos. 90 minutes later, when they finally returned, only 20% of their guests were still waiting to celebrate with them. If the guests of honor are gone too long from a reception, many guests will perceive this as a green light to make their exit.

Photojournalists Vs. Posers

Photographers who specialize in the popular photojournalist approach tend to stay out of the way as they attempt to capture candid moments and emotions. Photographers who prefer to pose their shots can vary in their level of involvement. For example, some will motion from

a distance for the bride and groom to both look at the camera during their First Dance, while others may make them stop dancing, and then place their hands, adjust their leg position and the direction their faces are turned before lining up the camera and taking the shot. The latter example is entirely realistic and can have a dramatic impact on the flow of your reception, especially if this type of over-involved "poser" has to set up each and every shot this way throughout your reception. Preferences over posed photos and photojournalistic photos are completely personal and you should strive to secure the photographer whose style and results will match your expectations. However, if their photos are almost all posed shots, and look stiff or contrived, ask them how involved they get in setting up their shots.

Video Re-Enactments

Just as some photographers can be known to spend too much time setting up overly posed photos, there are also some videographers who can cause similar delays of their own by insisting on shooting 2 or 3 additional "takes" of a memorable moment. Perhaps they failed to get the footage they needed the first time, or maybe they are trying to get different angles to simulate a 2 camera shoot. Regardless of why they may choose to do this, it will not only cost you time and slow down the pace or your reception's flow, but it can also turn a spontaneous moment into one that now feels contrived and uncomfortable. If your cake cutting, which might last 5 minutes, turns into 15 minutes of filming "video re-enactments," your guests may begin to lose interest sooner than you'd like. Be sure to ask your videographer about whether or not they make a habit of shooting "video re-enactments." You should also check with your entertainment to make sure they will keep your videographer informed before starting any activities that may need to be captured on video.

Tick Tock, Tick Tock

Another common way your photographer's service can negatively impact the entertaining flow of your reception is if their contracted service time ends much earlier then the duration of your reception. If the photographer begins pressuring your entertainment to "speed things up" so they can finish on time per their contract, this can lead to an agenda that begins to feel rushed. If you prefer not to pay to have your photographer stay until reception ends, at least schedule them to stay until all of your festivities have been completed without having to rush. But, if you can afford to hire a photographer who will stay until your reception ends, I would highly recommend it. I can't tell you how many creative, fun and unexpected moments I have seen occur during the last hour of dancing at a reception that were never captured by the photographer. This can be especially disappointing if you have a festive sendoff planned and no one is there to professionally capture those moments on film.

Blinded by the Light

One of the more common problems that can be created by the videographer you select is the lighting they will need to properly capture their footage. Most of the professionals use camera lights that can be adjusted from dim to bright. But if the videographer has a camera light that only features one setting, extra bright, not only will many of your images get washed out, but it can also scare people away from your dance floor. I have seen the Father of the Bride coming out to the dance floor for the Father/Daughter Dance with his hand shielding his eyes because the videographer's light was too bright. Then there's videographers filming the guests dancing from less than a foot away (attempting to get American Bandstand style footage) with a light that is so bright that it caused some of the guests to leave the dance floor. The real pros use the best tools and they know how to use them to capture the footage they need without intruding on or disrupting your celebration.

Flexible Team Players

If your photographer and/or videographer are not flexible team players, miscommunication problems may result. If your photographer has plans to do a large group photo, but doesn't communicate in advance with your entertainment about this, a smooth-flowing agenda may need to be suddenly disrupted to accommodate such a request. By working with your entertainment and communicating about these details before your big day, not only will the photographer and/or videographer get the shots they want, but their requests will also be incorporated into your agenda in a manner that will keep your reception's overall pace on track. Be sure to ask your photographer and/or videographer if they will be willing to discuss these details in advance with your entertainment.

Conclusion

As with any talent-based profession, there are professional photographers and videographers and there are some who are less than professional. The pros will dress appropriately, return your calls and treat your needs with the respect and timeliness you deserve. They will be passionate about doing a great job for you because their livelihood and word of mouth referrals depend on it. They will be experienced in working with your other vendors as a team player and capturing the special moments that you will be able to look back on for years to come. They will definitely cost more than the part-timer who is just looking for some extra income, but their results and service will always deliver the better value. If capturing your memories on photos and video is important to you, don't cut corners. Choose a true professional you can count on to document your day without hampering the success of your reception experience.

"Choose a true professional you can count on to document your day without hampering the success of your reception experience."

CHAPTER 7

AUDITIONING FOR TALENT
Filling Your Primary Supporting Roles:
Choosing a Minister, a Band, a DJ/MC,
or a Wedding Entertainment Director™

When the buzz is growing in Hollywood about a new movie that is getting ready to begin production, it can usually be attributed to the lead actors and the primary supporting actors who have been secured to star in the picture. The two of you are already filling the lead roles as the Bride and Groom at your ceremony and reception, but a strong team of primary supporting actors can also contribute greatly to the overall success of your day, while also helping the two of you to carry off an Oscar® worthy performance as the graceful hosts of an unforgettable celebration. Your primary supporting actors will be your wedding minister and your entertainment. In this chapter, we will explore the options you will face and the things that need to be seriously considered when selecting these crucial vendors.

"Dearly Beloved..."

The person you select to officiate your wedding ceremony may help you to create a uniquely personalized ceremony or they may prefer to use the same script and outline that they have used for the last 20 years. They may speak in a manner that is polished, eloquent and conversational, or they may speak in a droning manner with no feeling whatsoever. If you've ever sat through a ceremony that was officiated without feeling or emotion, then you already know how vital the role played by your officiate will be in making your ceremony meaningful and memorable.

There are many different options to consider when you are selecting your wedding minister. One of the first concerns is examining both of your religious backgrounds and then determining what will work best for both of you and your families. If you have both been raised Catholic and your families would be strongly opposed to a ceremony that isn't held in a local Catholic church, then your options may be limited. If one of you has been raised Protestant and the other is Jewish, then a professional wedding minister who can balance a multi-cultural ceremony may be a better fit. For a non-religious, yet personalized ceremony, some couples have even approached a friend or relative to serve as their minister. Many states offer a "minister-for-the-day" license that can give anyone the legal ability to perform a marriage ceremony.

In his seminar titled, "Create Your Perfect Wedding Ceremony!," the Rev. Clint Hufft said "There are 4 kinds of Wedding Ceremonies. The first is the Heart Wedding, which takes place when you fall in love

with each other and realize that you want to spend the rest of your lives together. The second is the Legal Wedding, which is a contract between the Bride and Groom that is recognized and approved by your local government. This is when your Marriage License is signed by both of you and your witnesses after the Minister has fulfilled the legal requirements of your Ceremony. The third is the Social Wedding, which begins when you send out your invitations and commences when your closest family and friends arrive to witness your union and join in your celebration. And the fourth is the Religious Wedding, which can be done in a church, a synagogue, or even in a park. The point of the Religious Wedding is that your commitment will not just be to each other, but before God as well. It should also be noted, however, that all 4 kinds of Wedding Ceremonies must fulfill the requirements of the Legal Wedding to be recognized as a legally binding marriage ceremony. So, be sure to research the legal requirements for getting married in your state."[1]

After examining these 4 kinds of Wedding Ceremonies, you should have a pretty clear idea about the kind of Minister you'll need. If your desire is to just have a Legal Wedding, this can be done by a Judge at the courthouse or by an Elvis impersonator in Las Vegas. If having a Religious Wedding is important to you, then your Pastor or Rabbi may be your first and/or only option for your Officiate. Regardless of where your priorities lie with the style of ceremony you are looking to create, you should always be able to find a professional minister available that can work with you to create a personalized ceremony. These questions may help you to identify the best minister for your needs:

◆ Can we see your set ceremony?

Most Wedding Ministers have a set ceremony outline, or variations thereof, that they follow. They should be more than happy to share their set ceremony with you so you can discuss the order and your personal expectations in great detail. If the Minister is not willing to share their set ceremony with you, this should be cause for concern. After all, how will you know that they won't say or do something during your ceremony that would not fit your desires, unless you can see it and discuss it ahead of time? If they offer you a wide variety of set ceremonies from which to choose, you are most likely in good hands.

◆ Can we make personalized adjustments to your set ceremony?

If the minister is open to adjusting their set routine to accommodate your personalized tastes and ideas for the ceremony, their answer will be an emphatic, "yes". If they are unwilling to consider making adjustments to their set ceremony, you will have to weigh whether this minister can still create the kind of ceremony you want. You might have to settle for what they "always do" instead of getting the personalization you were expecting. It really comes down to your priorities. If you want to create a personalized ceremony, then you should hold out for a minister who can and will accommodate your requests.

The Best
Wedding
Reception
...Ever!

◆ Can we make adjustments to the wording in your set ceremony?

Some couples like the traditional pronouncement of "man and wife" while others might find that wording offensive. Some couples may prefer vows that end with "as long as we both shall live" over vows that end with "until death do us part." Don't be afraid to raise these issues with your minister. The traditional phrase, "If anyone can give a reason why these two should not be joined together, speak now or forever hold your peace", is very rarely used these days. But one couple used it in a lakeside ceremony to add some humor to their wedding. By adjusting it slightly, their minister said, "If anyone can give a reason why these two should not be joined together, please feel free to go jump in the lake."

◆ Can we see video footage of you performing a wedding ceremony?

If you have the opportunity to see video footage of your minister performing a wedding ceremony, it would be well worth your time to review such footage. This will enable you to see and hear first hand how they speak and carry themselves when officiating a wedding ceremony. Listen to the tenor in their voice. Do they sound like they are happy for the bride and groom, or do they sound like they've said these same words so often that the words have lost all meaning and value? Watch their expressions and body language. Do they look poised? Are they smiling? Or do they look dispassionate? Keep in mind that your minister is setting the tone for the rest of your celebration. At one ceremony, I witnessed a minister who delivered the entire ceremony in just 3 minutes flat. The parents were very disappointed and the bride and groom were caught completely off guard. If they had asked to see some video footage, they might have selected a more polished minister.

◆ Will you be able to attend our Rehearsal?

Many professional ministers are not always available to attend your Rehearsal. If having them present at your Rehearsal is important to you, be sure to ask them up front before you make your final selection. Keep in mind that some of them may be willing to attend your Rehearsal, but you may also incur an additional fee as a result.

The Ceremony Minstrels

If you are thinking about hiring live musicians to play the music for your Wedding Ceremony, there are several important things to consider.

◆ Can the singers really sing?

There's nothing worse than a singer who is off key and doesn't know the words during a wedding ceremony. Ask to hear a demo tape, ask to view a demo video, or ask to see an audition before making any final decisions about singers during your ceremony. Also, make sure they have their instrumental music CD if there will be no live musicians.

◆ Will they have your ceremony sheet music in a separate binder?

Some musicians bring one large binder that holds the sheet music for every song they can play. But if the actual ceremony songs are not in a separate binder, there may be lengthy delays between the song for the seating of the Mothers and the beginning of the Wedding Party's Processional as the musicians flip through their entire sheet music library to find the next song. This delay can be easily avoided if they have taken the time to prepare a separate folder in advance, featuring just your ceremony music selections.

◆ Can they wrap up a song early if needed?

A common delay in wedding ceremonies occurs when the live musicians are unable to wrap up a song early and thus have to finish the entire piece of sheet music, while the Bride is standing in front of the Minister and everyone is ready for the ceremony to commence. Be sure to ask if the musicians you are considering have the confidence, skill, and experience to wrap up your ceremony selections at the appropriate time.

◆ How many guests will be attending the Ceremony?

Depending on your guest count, your musicians may need additional sound support and amplification. If you have over 300 guests, a string quartet may not be able to create enough volume all on their own. If you have singers and/or other musicians, they may need additional microphones and an extra person managing the audio mixer. If they don't have the equipment and/or personnel to meet these needs, you will need to seek out professional audio support.

The iPod Wedding

Apple's popular portable digital music player, the iPod, has been making the news quite a bit lately when it comes to weddings. On August 17th, 2005, National Public Radio featured a radio news story on iPod Weddings[2]. On September 20th, 2005, CNET New.com published a story on their web site about iPod Weddings[3]. The Chicago Tribune published a story on August 13th, 2006 about iPod Weddings[4]. Even the Wall Street Journal, on August 24th, 2006, published an article on iPod Weddings[5]. The common theme between the stories were brides and grooms who didn't want a "Cheesy DJ" to ruin their wedding day, while also being able to maintain complete control over the music selections at their celebrations. For the financially strapped wedding reception, an iPod may be a highly viable option. But the one factor most of these stories have not covered was the actual end results of using an iPod to provide the music for a ceremony and/or reception celebration. The title of this chapter is "Auditioning For Talent" and talent is the one component that Apple will never be able to program into their iPods. A truly unforgettable celebration requires the talent and skill to not only play the right music at just the right moment, but it also requires the ability to guide and direct your celebration while keeping your guests informed and involved. No iPod will ever be able to do that.

The glorification of the iPod Wedding option is a symptom of the "just music" mentality that has permeated the entire wedding industry's various forms of media. By telling brides that they just need music, instead of properly informing them about the value and services provided by skilled and talented entertainment, they have paved the way for iPod Weddings to be given serious consideration by today's brides.

Cosmopolitan Magazine has even contributed to this misinformation. Their June, 2004 issue featured an article titled "25 Tips You'll Never Find in a Bridal Magazine."[6] Tip number 20 was titled, "Enlist your Own Deejay" and suggested that brides should, "Make a personal play list by loading an MP3 player or iPod (get a friend or hire an amateur deejay to man it) with songs you dig."

An iPod is a glorified Jukebox. If background music playing on shuffle will sufficiently take care of your reception's entertainment needs, then by all means, build a play-list, rent some sound equipment, and save yourself some money. For an extended cocktail hour style of reception without the traditional formalities or expectations for dancing, an iPod may be exactly what you need.

But if you have certain songs that you need played for the various moments of your ceremony and/or reception, if you want your guests to feel involved in your celebration, and if creating fun dancing is important to you, then you should seriously consider hiring an entertainment professional to meet your needs.

In her August 13th, 2006 article, written for the Chicago Tribune, titled, "The do-it-yourself wedding soundtrack"[4], Angel Rozas reported on an iPod Wedding she attended. In the article, she pointed out the real downside to using an iPod for your wedding ceremony when she shared the following anecdote:

"The ceremony was halted midway through when the "iPod attendant," as he was listed in the wedding program, could not figure out how to stop a song from playing.

Steve (the groom), who was holding his bride's hand, turned to make the international "Turn it off!" sign, sliding his finger across his throat. Another friend jumped up to help. No luck. With 70 pairs of eyes on him, the groom left the bride and walked over to fix the iPod.

It wasn't the only glitch. The start of the wedding had been delayed until someone could figure out how to cue the right song for the bride to march down the aisle. During the reception, the iPod's downloads were playing at uneven volumes, forcing another friend to run back and forth to the music table to adjust the sound."

When asked why they opted to use an iPod for their ceremony and reception, the groom in the story responded by saying:

"Why do we want to pay some dopey deejay $3,000 to press play on a CD changer when we can spend that money on something more important than that?"

One has to ask why this groom thought a $3,000 DJ would only be pressing play on a CD changer? Could it be because so many books and magazines have only been suggesting that brides and grooms hire "music," instead of opening their eyes to the full scope of services that are regularly provided by professional wedding entertainers?

On August 31st, 2006, DJARadio.com (a podcast "talk radio station" for professional mobile DJs) featured an interview by Bill James on "Chat Rash" with Raymond Flandez, the author of the August 24th, 2006 Wall Street Journal article titled "More couples program music iPods for wedding music."[5] When Bill James questioned Mr. Flandez about any feedback he may have received regarding possible detrimental results from using only an iPod at a reception, Mr. Flandez said...

"My roommate went to a wedding this summer and he was just like stunned that there was just an iPod there, but no one was dancing on the dance floor. ... DJs keep the flow going and read the crowd. That's an important aspect of what DJs do and that's going to be something that's going to be missed when you're just playing with an iPod." [7]

He went on to reveal that his original article had included these observations, but they were cut from the final article due to space restrictions.

Hopefully, by the time you finish this chapter, you will have a very clear understanding of the various types of entertainment services that are available. But don't be fooled into thinking that an iPod can create an entertaining reception. Because after all...iPods...only play music.

How About That Band?

Live Bands have been providing music and entertainment at wedding celebrations since the invention of musical instruments. Some bands are great, many are best described as typical, and others are just plain awful.

If you are considering hiring a Live Band to provide your wedding entertainment, here are some important benefits to consider as you prepare to make your decision.

- ✚ Live Bands can play music really well.
- ✚ Live Bands can bring a lot of energy into a room.
- ✚ Live Bands can do medleys and extended jam sessions of songs.

> **"Live Bands are second to none when it comes to creating energy that can get your crowd up and moving on the dance floor."**

Live Bands are second to none when it comes to creating energy that can get your crowd up and moving on the dance floor. When they see that a song is getting a large reaction from your guests, they can often keep that song going longer than normal. Many of them are skilled at creating medleys that blend from one song and/or genre into another on the fly. They can also help you create a specific environment. If you want to create a swing/big band theme, a 10 piece orchestra with a crooner style singer might be just the ticket.

However, there are some important things you should seriously consider before selecting a Live Band.

◆ How will you perform my special songs?

Every Live Band will play the songs you have selected in their own way. Even the best Cover Bands are just imitating the original artists. Some bands will take a song that was made popular as an Oldie and perform it as a Reggae song instead. When you selected the song for your First Dance, what prompted your decision? Did you select the song because it reminds you of the time when the two of you first met? Did you select the song because the lyrics clearly communicate your current feelings for each other? Whatever contributed to your decisions for all of the special songs you are looking forward to hearing on your wedding day, you should be aware that a Live Band will not play the songs exactly as you remember them. The instrumentation may be similar, the vocals may even be close to the original artist's recording, but a Band will still perform your songs their way. Ask to see a demo or an audition of the Band performing your First Dance selection. This opportunity might also give you a better understanding of their unique style.

◆ How many songs and genres can you currently perform?

This question will help you identify if the Live Band you are considering has the range of music needed to truly make your party happen. Some bands are limited to only one or two specific genres. If they are not up to date with the current hit songs for dancing, they might not be able to appeal to your younger guests. If they are strong on the new music, but are limited on the classics and the oldies, your older guests might feel left out. If you are creating a theme, then genre limitations might be acceptable for your needs.

◆ Who will be making the announcements at our reception?

Just because someone can sing, doesn't necessarily mean they are qualified to serve as your spokesperson. If you have ever watched American Idol, then you know that there are lots of people who think they can sing well, but really can't. The same can be said about the specialized talent and skill that is required to be an exceptional Master of Ceremonies at a wedding reception. When any good performer, whether they are a singer, an MC, or an actor, does what they do extremely well,

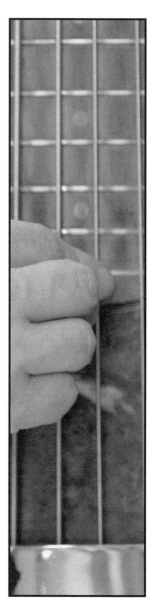

it is commonly perceived as being reasonably easy to do. However, it is not easy to be an exceptional singer or an exceptional actor. And being exceptional as a Master of Ceremonies is no easy task either. Just ask Billy Crystal why he spends several months preparing to host the Academy Awards. Yet, when Billy Crystal does host, he not only makes it look easy, but he typically outshines the other regular hosts.

Being a great musician takes years of training and practice combined with unique talent and specialized skills. However, all of this work and talent may not matter much when it's time to announce your wedding party's grand entrance. When considering a Live Band, it is imperative that you take the time to find out what training has been taken by the band's MC to serve effectively as your spokesperson. Ask them to make sample announcements as an audition. Everyone auditions the music, but how many people overlook the capabilities of the MC to inform your guests in an appropriate and polished manner? If their announcements are generic in nature, such as referring to you as "The Bride & Groom" or "The Happy Couple", instead of using your first names, then your guests will experience a very impersonal presentation from the MC. Don't wait until your wedding day to find out that your singer isn't qualified to serve as your spokesperson.

◆ Can we see uncut video footage of announcements you have made at weddings in the past?

Be sure to ask for video footage of the Band in action. If they provide you with footage, it will undoubtedly show guests dancing and enjoying themselves as the Band is playing some great tunes. But watch carefully and look for the special moments in the reception that will require clear, concise and polished announcements. If they are only showing you edited footage that leaves out their announcements, then insist on seeing an audition of how they will announce your special moments.

◆ What training have you taken to develop your skills as an MC?

There are many opportunities available for developing the skills required to be a polished Master of Ceremonies. One can join a local meeting of Toastmasters International or take a class on public speaking. Acting, Voice Over, and/or Comedy workshops can also be quite helpful. The point is someone who is serious about properly fulfilling the role of Master of Ceremonies at your reception will invest the necessary time to become truly exceptional. Only amateurs "wing" it.

◆ What is your policy on taking breaks during our reception?

Be sure to explore the band's policy on breaks before making a final decision. Playing live music is hard work. It can be downright exhausting. But most Bands have a solution for this predictable dilemma. The solution is called break-time. Imagine your dance floor is fully packed with friends and family members who are dancing to their heart's content when the band leader suddenly announces, "Ummm, folks, we're gonna take a break...we'll be back in about 15 minutes." Now what?

What happens next may vary depending on the band you are considering. They may take a break with no music playing for the next 15 minutes, and while nothing is happening, many of your guests may decide that it is time leave. They may throw on a background CD and just let it play unattended during their break. This option may also cause many of your guests to leave early. They may even have a DJ on site to play requests during their breaks, and depending on their DJ's skill level, this may keep the guests dancing or they may still start heading for the door.

Is taking a break the only option? Not if you hire a Great Wedding Band, a Talented DJ, or a Wedding Entertainment Director™. A Great Wedding Band will bring along extra musicians so their band members can take individual breaks throughout your reception while the rest of the band plays on. This solution keeps the energy going, but as you might expect, a Great Wedding Band will most likely cost much more than a Typical Wedding Band. A Talented DJ and/or a Wedding Entertainment Director™ will also keep the music going non-stop without ever taking a break because they play pre-recorded music and will also often work with an assistant.

If the Band you are considering has a break-time policy that will impact the success of your reception in a negative way, you might want to re-consider hiring them. Your reception is only going to happen once. If they are not using one of the simple solutions outlined above, then allow me to suggest that you look instead for a Great Wedding Band, a Talented DJ, or a Wedding Entertainment Director™.

◆ Do you have extra band members available so breaks can be rotated?

If the Band you are considering does not have additional musicians that can rotate in and out for individual breaks, then you should expect the Band to have a break-time policy as described above. Don't be afraid to ask them how they will keep your celebration going while they are taking a break.

◆ What is your policy on meals?

Some bands may insist on being fed during your reception. Some may even request being fed the same meal as your guests, which can lead to an unexpected increase on your catering bill. Be sure to ask your catering contact if they typically provide a regular meal or a less expensive "vendor meal" for the band members.

◆ Do you have a DJ on staff to play recorded music during your breaks?

If the Band's solution to the break-time issue is to supply their own DJ who will spin tunes during their breaks, be sure to ask for references and

video footage of their DJ in action. Keep in mind that truly Talented DJs will rarely ever give up their prime dates to play band breaks. So the question needs to be asked…can the Band's DJ measure up to the task?

◆ How will you prevent Dead Air from occurring at my reception?

One of the worst mistakes you can make on radio is Dead Air. Dead Air is when the cue for the next commercial, song or announcement is missed, and the listener's hear nothing at all for several seconds or even minutes. Dead Air is also a serious issue when considering a Live Band. If you ask to view a demo video, you can rest assured that there will be no Dead Air left for you to see. So be proactive and ask to see an uncut video of the Band in action so you can watch how well they transition from one song to the next.

A Typical Wedding Band will commonly allow several seconds or even minutes of Dead Air between songs as they discuss which song to play next and maybe even re-tune their instruments. Sometimes they will even allow Dead Air after the toasts or some other event where well-timed music would have made for a much better transition. A Great Wedding Band will be ready to play after each special event and they will keep the music going seamlessly without taking breaks or pausing to determine which song they should play next. A Talented DJ and/or a Wedding Entertainment Director™ will also deliver a performance free of Dead Air as they are playing pre-recorded music and they have usually helped to plan out the entire agenda, so they are fully aware of each important cue.

Dead Air can really put a damper on the dancing at a reception. Imagine a great song ending and as the crowd is applauding, the Typical Wedding Band begins to discuss amongst themselves what song they should play next. While they are busy talking, the Dead Air becomes uncomfortable and the guests, who are now just standing on the dance floor, begin to walk back to their tables. Just as they reach their seats, the Band strikes up with another song and some of the guests come back and begin to dance again. Now, repeat that process several times. Soon, your guests will begin to grow tired of the Dead Air between the songs and many of them will begin to head for the door. So insist on seeing uncut footage of your Band before deciding whether they will be providing the entertainment at your reception.

◆ What responsibility do you take for directing the pacing and flow of my reception's agenda?

When it comes to managing the pacing and flow of your reception's agenda, who's directing? This subject will be covered in greater detail in Chapter 8: "Nominating the Best Director." A Live Band will be able to play music, and they might even make the announcements for you, but will they be able to play their instruments and guide and direct your reception events at the same time? Who will make sure that the cake knife is at the cake table before your cake cutting is announced? Who will let your parents know in advance to be ready for their special dances with you? A good wedding coordinator might, and a Wedding Entertainment Director™ will for sure, but a Typical Wedding Band won't have the time, manpower, or skill to direct your reception because their job is primarily about playing the music.

Ask the Band how they manage the details of your agenda and if they say they will direct your reception's events, ask them to tell you how. If this is a service they regularly offer, then they will most likely be able to verify that they do this by producing a detailed reception direction checklist. If they cannot produce such a checklist, then they are most likely winging it and hoping nothing will go wrong. Experience has shown us that those who "wing it," tend to run into problems more often than those that are prepared and are double-checking the details.

◆ How will you communicate with the other vendors about my agenda while you are performing?

It can be hard to communicate clearly with a Band while they are performing. Their music is loud and they are in the middle of performing. But a Great Wedding Band will undoubtedly have an assistant who can discuss agenda details with the other vendors and then effectively cue the Band when needed. If your Band does not have someone filling this role on their behalf, they most likely will be relying on your coordinator and/or catering director to keep them informed about changes in the agenda. If the coordinator and/or catering director are not keeping the Band properly informed, you may run into more occurrences of dead air as the Band is left to figure out for themselves what they should be doing or playing next.

◆ Can your volume levels be turned down if requested?

Some bands start off loud, stay loud and then just get louder. Be sure to ask the Band if they are willing to turn their volume down if and when it is requested. If your guests have to shout to carry on a conversation during dinner, the music is too loud and many of your guests will be turned off by the Band.

◆ What can you tell me about your service and performance that sets you apart from all the rest?

If the Band cannot effectively answer this question, then they are most likely just a Typical Wedding Band. Will you be content with a "typical" overall reception entertainment experience? Can something that is just "typical" create something that is truly remarkable? Would you expect a "typical" caterer to deliver the best quality food and service? Would you expect a "typical" florist to create decorations that are breathtakingly creative and original? Then why would you expect anything more than "typical" from a Typical Wedding Band?

"Be sure to ask the Band if they are willing to turn their volume down if and when it is requested."

If you would prefer for your guests to experience a reception that is exceptional, first-class, marvelous, outstanding, phenomenal, remarkable, extraordinary, sophisticated and wonderful, then you might be looking for something more than typical. It is possible that you could find a Typical Wedding Band that also happens to be able to deliver a high quality service and level of performance, but chances are they won't be just a Typical Wedding Band for long. A Great Wedding Band will be able to communicate clearly about the facets of their service and performance that set them apart from all the rest.

The DJ/MC (Disc Jockey/Master of Ceremonies)

Disc Jockeys have been providing music and entertainment at wedding celebrations since the early 1970's, when they first emerged as a cheaper alternative to Live Bands. When Disc Jockeys first began entertaining at receptions, their primary focus was on playing pre-recorded music for the dancing. Some companies expanded their services by offering disco lighting. Some expanded their services by hiring additional DJs so they could cover multiple clients and events simultaneously. And some expanded their services to include the Master of Ceremonies duties. In Canada, some Disc Jockeys are just now starting to offer Master of Ceremonies services because culturally, the Best Man or a family friend has usually been asked to fill that role. In the 1990's, some Disc Jockeys expanded their services by becoming "party motivators" who were skilled at teaching and leading creative group dances. Others expanded their services by offering more assistance with the planning and overall direction of the reception's pacing and flow. And finally, some DJs expanded their performance services by offering uniquely personalized entertainment that is designed to keep the focus on the bride and groom.

With all of this variety available, it is disconcerting to note that the overall perceptions about Disc Jockeys in regards to wedding celebrations are typically negative. Words like "cheesy" or "obnoxious" are often used to describe bad DJ entertainment. Part of this overall negative perception might be related to the fact that a large majority of Mobile Disc Jockeys in the United States are currently DJing as a sideline business while working in an unrelated full-time career during the week. With limited time to invest into their performance and deliver their services, many of them are stuck in a cycle of mediocrity. But there are Talented DJs available if you know how and where to find them.

If you are considering hiring a Disc Jockey/Master of Ceremonies to provide the entertainment at your wedding reception, here are some important benefits to consider as you prepare to make your decision.

+ Disc Jockeys can mix pre-recorded music really well.
+ Disc Jockeys can play a wide variety of music genres.
+ Disc Jockeys can keep your celebration flowing smoothly.

Disc Jockeys have the advantage of being able to play just about any genre of music you've requested, while being able to change gears on a moment's notice to adjust to your guest's reactions. This difficult to master art form is known as "reading the crowd". A really Talented DJ will not only read your crowd, but they will also lead and direct your guests with both their music selections and their announcements. The best entertainers will work with your other vendors to make sure everything is going smoothly behind the scenes so you don't have to be concerned about what will be happening next. A Talented DJ can help you create a fun reception that will keep your guests entertained for the duration of your celebration.

However, there are some important things you should seriously consider before selecting a Disc Jockey/Master of Ceremonies.

◆ Is being a DJ/MC your full-time career?

According to a 2004 DJ Times survey, 64% of Wedding DJs work on a part-time basis while holding down regular weekday jobs[8]. Will your photographer be a part-timer who isn't qualified enough to do wedding photography as their chosen profession? Will your catering be done by somebody who just enjoys making food for large groups of people on the weekends, but their real career is as an accountant? Based on the ratio of part-timers who DJ at weddings, it's a pretty safe bet that an Average Wedding DJ is also a part-timer whose loyalties, priorities and time are divided between your reception and their regular, 9 to 5 job. It's been said that there are no waiters in L.A. and New York, only actors who are between acting jobs. But have you ever seen an exceptional movie actor who is still working full-time as a waiter? The best rise to the top and turn their passion into their career. But based on the stats, the Average Wedding DJ may not have the time or the skills to give your reception the full-time attention and service your day deserves.

One of the reasons given by part-time hobbyist Wedding DJs for not being full-time, professionals, is their belief that they won't be able to replace their income and medical benefits which are currently provided by their full-time, regular job. So how do full-time wedding photographers do it? How do full-time wedding florists do it? They charge a professional fee that will provide them with the income and medical benefits they need, in addition to covering their annual business expenses and self-employment taxes. Because such a large number of Wedding DJs are part-time hobbyists, it's probably not too surprising to note that their average pricing is typically set too low to provide the necessary income needed to make this their full-time career.

Another excuse for being part-time is the idea that they just really enjoy being a Wedding DJ. It's fun and therefore, they don't care about making it their career or earning a professional income. But most who approach being a Wedding DJ as their full-time profession also enjoy what they do, in fact they are usually downright passionate about it. And because it

Auditioning
For
Talent

is their full-time career, they have more time to invest in improving their services and/or their performance. They can afford to take time off to attend industry trade shows and workshops. They are available to meet with you or return your calls during the weekdays. And because being a Wedding DJ is their career, they have more pressure to deliver the best performance and service possible. In comparison, a part-time, hobbyist Wedding DJ can get by delivering just an average level of services and/or performance because they still have the income from their full-time, regular job to fall back on. This may not always be the case, but "Average Is As Average Does".

If the DJ you are considering says that they are just as good as any full-time DJ, even though they only DJ as a sideline, you should ask yourself why they haven't already been able to go full-time themselves? The full-time DJ has not only developed their talent and their skill to a professional level, but they have also developed enough demand for their services to be able to make being a DJ their full-time profession. Someone who claims to be just as good should have no problem achieving the same results. Now you may find a rare part-time DJ who truly delivers exceptional service, but chances are if they are that good, they won't remain part-time for very long. The majority of the part-time DJs you will encounter, however, will most likely only be able to deliver an amateur level of performance at best.

Ask the DJ/MC how many weddings they personally perform each year. Keep in mind that a larger number (like over 100) might not necessarily imply better experience, but rather just more experience doing weddings that may likely be too similar for your unique tastes and desires. Multiply the number of weddings they cover annually by their average wedding rate. If the figure you come up with is less than $50,000 in total gross annual income, keep in mind that after business expenses and self-employment taxes, they are probably making the equivalent of what they would earn at a minimum wage job. If working as a DJ is not their primary source of income, it is reasonable to question whether they will be completely committed to giving you the very best service possible. Someone whose livelihood truly depends on giving you their very best performance at your wedding reception, will most likely do just that.

◆ Are your prices below average, average, or above average and why?

Regardless of what their pricing may be, a DJ/MC should always be able to clearly communicate the reasons for their pricing and the value that is provided in their overall services. If their pricing is below average, they may be just getting into the business, or they might be DJing as a sideline. Another answer may be that they are not able or willing to deliver an average quality of service and/or performance and have thus settled into a price range that is therefore appropriate. If their price is average, perhaps they are comfortable delivering just an average quality of service. There is a remote possibility that they may be a truly Talented DJ who is just unaware of their ranking and true value, but it is doubtful that they would remain in that price range for long. If their pricing is above average, chances are pretty good that you are speaking with a Talented DJ who has seen increased demand for their unique talents, which has enabled them to charge a premium fee for their services. There is the remote possibility that you might encounter an average or below average DJ who is trying to charge more than they are actually worth, but if they fail to deliver a value to their clients, they will begin to lose referrals and their prices will have to be adjusted back down to a figure that is more in line with their actual value.

When considering hiring entertainment for a wedding reception, the ability to make an informed decision can often be influenced by average pricing. Due to the large majority of Wedding DJs being only part-time hobbyists instead of full-time professionals, it's pretty safe to say that the average pricing you will encounter will be indicative of Wedding DJs who don't take their business seriously enough to make it their full-time career. In fact, in a DJ Times survey, 81% of the DJs surveyed make less than $46,000 per year[8]. When you then speak with a full-time professional, their price may seem high in comparison to the average pricing you have already encountered. At that point, you will have an important decision to make. Will a Wedding DJ who offers average pricing deliver anything more than average results? Will spending more on a full-time, professional Wedding DJ be a better value?

In the service world, the most expensive services are quite commonly the ones who are providing their clients with the best overall value. Within 2 miles of my home, I have the option to get my hair cut at a Barber Shop for around $6, at a large chain store for around $15, or at a nice salon for around $40. All three will cut my hair, but I get the best service and personal attention at the salon. My stylist, Rocky, not only takes the time to make sure my hair turns out exactly how I expected, but he is also personable and he takes a sincere interest in my business and my life. I have yet to ever see a bride getting her hair done at a Barber Shop or at a large chain store on her wedding day. Brides know that on their wedding day, their hair has to be perfect, and so they go to the salon. They will probably spend more than they normally would for just a basic cut and style as well. If you are looking for the best DJ entertainment for your reception, seek out the DJ who is priced above the average and then ask them why. Their response should help you determine if the value they will provide will be worth the added investment.

In reality, all Wedding DJs do many of the same things, but how those things are done determines whether you are dealing with a Talented DJ, a professional Wedding Entertainment Director™, or an Average Wedding DJ. Pricing for Wedding DJs is tied directly to their skill and talent levels, because the top performers will always see increased demand thus allowing them to charge increasingly higher fees. But an Average Wedding DJ will not see as much increased demand and will thus remain stuck in the range of average pricing.

"Will spending more on a full-time, professional Wedding DJ be a better value?"

◆ Will I be guaranteed to get the DJ that I want and will their name be listed on the Contract?

If the DJ is unwilling to list the DJ you have selected (whether it be them or one of their employees) by name on the Contract, then perhaps they are not willing to guarantee who will actually be the DJ at your reception. This should be cause for alarm. If you develop a good rapport with a DJ, but on the day of your reception, you are greeted by one of that DJ's subordinates with no advance warning, you may be in for a bumpy ride. Unfortunately, some DJs treat wedding receptions like "gigs." They will book as many "gigs" as they can get, and then send out an employee or a sub-contractor with a story about why the often better qualified owner was not available. The tactic is called "Bait & Switch" and it has been a blight on the DJ industry for far too long. You should expect and demand that the entertainer you choose be named and guaranteed in the Contract. Your reception entertainment is too important to be left in the hands of a total stranger.

◆ Are you a member of any industry trade associations?

Joining a trade association shows you that the DJ is committed to not only improving their own services, but it also demonstrates that they are committed to helping improve their industry as a whole. With the current negative perceptions that are facing the Mobile DJ industry, DJs who want to see a positive change in those perceptions are joining local and national trade associations to create a better future. Joining a trade association typically doesn't require any "proof" of their level of talent or professional status. But the desire to become more skilled or attain professional status is usually encouraged by such associations. What this means to brides is that being a trade association member is not verification of a DJs capabilities or quality of service, but it does show their commitment to ongoing education and training. As a former national President of the American Disc Jockey Association (ADJA), I highly endorse and recommend searching for prospective Disc Jockeys who are currently on their membership roster. The ADJA offers Local Chapters with monthly meetings and they provide educational content designed to help DJs of all skill levels improve their services and/or performances. You can look for an ADJA member in your area by visiting their web site (http://www.adja.org). There are many other local and national DJ associations available, and a simple Google search should help you locate any groups in your particular region.

◆ How can you assist me in planning out the agenda for my ceremony and/or reception?

A Talented DJ will be more than happy to help you create a detailed agenda for your ceremony and/or reception. They have learned through experience that a well-planned reception will always turn out much better than one that is disorganized and has only been thrown together at the last minute. Some DJs may tell you that they actually prefer to "wing it" when it comes to reception's agenda. What they are really telling you is that they don't have the time or the desire to help you plan your agenda. No one who is a quality entertainer ever just "wings it."

I learned this lesson first hand when I took a workshop on stand-up comedy and then performed at the Improv. The best comedians look like they are just spontaneously making up funny jokes while they are performing onstage. The reality is, they have often spent weeks and months and often years developing their unique routines and writing and re-writing their best material. By being well-prepared, they are able to deliver a performance that appears completely fresh and entertaining to their audience. The amount of time the DJ is willing to invest in helping you to create a detailed agenda will have a direct effect on how smoothly your reception will flow.

Some DJs will respond by offering you planning questionnaires to fill out in printed form or online. They may or may not offer a phone consultation on the week of your wedding to confirm the details you have provided on their forms. But keep in mind that this "hands off" approach may lead to you ending up with a reception agenda that feels like a run-of-the-mill, cookie-cutter celebration.

Talented DJs will most likely offer at least one face to face meeting and some will even offer two or more meetings as needed. By investing time with you to discuss your preferences and desires, they will be able to help you create a very personalized agenda for your ceremony and/or reception. They should provide you with forms or a list of questions to help you think about the type of reception events you want to do and don't want to do. They will be more than willing to offer helpful advice about the pacing and flow of your reception agenda.

◆ How many songs can I select for my ceremony and/or reception?

The correct answer should be "all of them," but you may get a variety of different answers to this question depending on the DJ you are interviewing at the time. Because this is your celebration, your input and opinions on the music selections should be given top priority. But some DJs will ask you to pick 10 songs for dancing and then insist that you just trust them to format the rest of the selections. If you trust this DJ, or have little to no opinion about your dancing music selections, then you may have found a good match for your needs. However, if you are particular about your music choices, then you may want to seek a DJ service that is willing to give you complete input over the music that will be played for your ceremony and/or reception.

There are 3 primary categories of music to consider when planning out your musical selections. The first category is your Background Music Selections. The music that will be playing as your guests are arriving for your ceremony will create a unique atmosphere. The same holds true for your cocktail hour music choices and the music that will play in the

background during the meal. This area more than just about any other tends to get swept under the rug by many DJs who prefer to play the same background mix at all of their receptions. Don't be afraid to insist on seeing a list of various types of background music from your DJ. If they are unable to produce such a list, then perhaps their background selections are severely limited or maybe they just prefer to make such decisions without your input.

The second category is your Special Moments Music Selections. The music that plays as you are walking down the aisle during your wedding ceremony should be determined by you and you alone. If you want the traditional "Bridal March" by Richard Wagner, then your DJ's next question should be, "which version would you prefer?" Whether it's your First Dance selection, or your choice for the Father/Daughter Dance, or the songs that are playing as you cut your cake or toss your bouquet, these are your moments and you should be able to choose the soundtrack that fits your personal style. Be sure to ask your DJ for a list of ceremony music suggestions as well as a list of suggested songs for your reception events. And feel free to come up with your own ideas for these moments as well. Music attaches itself to memories, and the songs you select for these moments will become a part of the memories you will carry with you for the rest of your life.

The third, and final category, is your Dancing Requests Music Selections. The music that plays during open dancing should absolutely rely on your input and preferences. But first, to be absolutely clear, your Disc Jockey should be entrusted to format your selections in order to create a mix of dancing music that will be appealing to the varied tastes and age groups represented at your reception. However, you should definitely be given the opportunity to weigh in with your top requests, your favorite artists, and your "do not play" list. Be sure to ask your DJ for a list of dancing music requests. If they balk at the notion and just ask you to write up your own list, they might be revealing that they prefer to use their own selections. This might be a good thing if they have a proven track record of creating energetic dancing at their past receptions. But it could also be a warning flag that they prefer to play the same 30 to 50 songs that they always play for dancing at all of their receptions. A Talented DJ should be able to incorporate your top requests and your favorite artists (provided the artist's songs are danceable) while avoiding the songs on your "do not play" list. A Talented DJ will also be able to filter in requests from your guests while occasionally mixing in songs they know will fit perfectly for your crowd in the moment. Be prepared to pick an average of 15-20 songs per each hour of open dancing, but don't be afraid to select more than needed so your DJ will have plenty of requests to work with when the time comes.

Bonus Chapters! As an added special bonus for purchasing this book, you can download 4 free Bonus Chapters, featuring the following music lists: Background Suggestions, Ceremony Suggestions, Reception Suggestions, and Dancing Requests. Simply register at:
TheBestWeddingReceptionEver.com

◆ What creative ideas can you share for making our wedding reception more fun in a personalized way?

This question will help you identify if the DJ believes that they just play music, or if they recognize the value of creating uniquely personalized entertainment. A DJ who still sees their job as "just music" will be more likely to treat your reception like a "gig" instead of seeking ways to create a personalized entertainment experience for you and your guests. A Talented DJ will be able to not only list out several unique and creative ideas, but they should also be able to help you develop ideas that will fit your reception perfectly. If they get stumped on this question, they are probably only familiar with delivering an average, cookie-cutter style of reception entertainment.

◆ What responsibility do you take for directing the pacing and flow of my reception's agenda?

Have you ever been a guest at a wedding reception that was moving along far too slowly? When the pace of a reception is not being properly directed, the guests will get restless and may become more inclined to consider leaving early. This subject will be covered in greater detail in Chapter 8: "Nominating the Best Director." Unfortunately, many DJs still show up to their events expecting someone else to direct the pacing and the flow. Perhaps they are counting on the coordinator for guidance. Maybe they are looking to the catering director for their cues. But if they are not actively trying to help maintain an entertaining flow, then your reception may be more likely to just drag along.

Because a smooth-flowing party will always result in more fun on the dance floor and more word-of-mouth referrals for your entertainment, many Talented DJs have become proactive (as opposed to reactive) about helping to direct the timing and flow of their receptions. They have discovered that when they share advance copies of your entertainment agenda with your location, your catering manager, your coordinator, your photographer, and your videographer, the rest of your team will be better informed and they will also be able to resolve any timing issues well before your big day. They have come to recognize that certain problems can be avoided if preparations are made to trouble-shoot such situations before they cause a delay in the flow of your reception.

If the DJ tells you that they regularly "coordinate" the details at their receptions, ask to see a copy of their direction checklists that they use to double-check details behind the scenes for their ceremonies and/or receptions. If they are unable to produce such checklists, then perhaps they are relying on a mental checklist or perhaps they are not really managing these details at all. Such a checklist should include things like: making sure the cake knife and cake server is on the cake table, making sure the parents are alerted discreetly before they will be needed for their special dances, verifying that the bride has her garter on before its time to begin the garter removal and toss. When details like these are

"If the DJ tells you that they regularly 'coordinate' the details at their receptions, ask to see a copy of their direction checklists"

managed effectively behind the scenes, the result will be a reception that flows very smoothly. This will only happen when someone is making sure the props and/or players are set in the right places at the right time. Unfortunately, the "coordination" that is offered by most Average DJs is typically more of a reactive approach to problem solving. This means they will "react" when something goes wrong and then try to solve it, rather than being proactive by trying to prevent such problems from occurring in the first place.

At one of my receptions a few years back, I was double checking some last minute details with the bride, and when I asked her if she had her garter on for later, she suddenly became distressed when she realized that her garter had been left at home. She was understandably upset at her predicament. I told her not to worry as I always carry a back-up garter for just such emergencies. Later that night, the garter removal and toss went off just as planned. The guests never knew that an unfortunate situation had been avoided thanks to careful preparation and direction.

◆ Are you familiar with our ceremony and/or reception location?

Because some locations can have unique challenges, it is very important that your entertainment be familiar with the space and room layout provided by your location. If the DJ has already worked at your location before, ask them if there were any unexpected problems with the room layout or with the location's preferred order or events. Listen as they explain how these obstacles were overcome or resolved.

At one ceremony and reception facility, the location would not allow the bride to take care of her own music and PA support through her entertainment vendor. Instead, they insisted on providing the PA support for the ceremony themselves and they only allowed the bride to hear her musical selections as played by their live pianist. When the bride pressed for more information, she was told that the owners of the facility felt that pre-recorded music was "schlocky" and made their location look bad. Because the bride was set on hearing her own pre-recorded selections for her ceremony, she cancelled with the location and moved to a facility that was more supportive of her desires. Knowing this, I will not sell my ceremony support services for this particular location, but I will also gladly share this story with any bride who is considering having her ceremony at this particular location in the future.

If the DJ has not worked at your location yet, be sure to ask if they will do a site visit before your big day. A Talented DJ will most likely insist on a site visit, and may even request to schedule it with you present so any challenges can be discussed and resolved on the spot, instead of turning into a problem during your reception. Some locations may require extra speakers. Some locations may require some help to make the room layout more entertaining. If your DJ discovers these issues for the first time on your wedding day, they may be short on extra speakers or they may not have time to make adjustments to the room layout.

A good entertainer will always make sure they are familiar with the "stage" and the "theater" where their performance will take place. An amateur will just show up and try to make do, or "wing it."

If your location has some unusual policies regarding the loading in of equipment, the volume levels, the set-up area for the DJ, or even the set order of reception events they prefer to execute, your DJ will need to know about such issues ahead of time. If your location's policies are too restrictive you may find some of the better quality entertainers choosing to pass on working at such facilities. One such facility in my area will not allow the entertainment to begin loading in until 1 hour before the doors open for the guests. They require the entertainment to set up in a back corner, some 45 feet away from the dance floor, making it harder to create the right volume levels for dancing while, at the same time, blasting out the guests who are unfortunate enough to be seated between the entertainment and the dance floor. This same facility will also require the bride and groom to cut their cake at the end of the meal, regardless of whether or not the bride and groom want to wait and cut their cake after some open dancing. This schedule is enforced so they can clear off the cake table for pitchers of water, iced tea, and lemonade. Because this location is so difficult to work with, myself and several other entertainers in my area will not book receptions at this particular facility.

If you have not yet found your location, ask your DJ which locations they would recommend and then ask them what makes those locations worth recommending. They might just have some insights about such locations that you might not be able to get from any other source.

◆ What training have you taken to develop your skills as an MC?

When considering a DJ, it is imperative that you take the time to find out what training the DJ has undertaken to serve effectively as your spokesperson. There are many opportunities available for developing the skills required to be a polished Master of Ceremonies. One can join a local meeting of Toastmasters International or take a class on public speaking. Acting, Voice Over, and/or Comedy workshops can also be quite helpful. Someone who is serious about properly fulfilling the role of Master of Ceremonies at your reception will invest the necessary time to become truly exceptional. Only amateurs wing it. Ask them to make sample announcements as an audition. If their audition announcements are generic in nature, such as referring to you as "The Bride & Groom" or "The Happy Couple," instead of using your first names, then your guests may very well experience an impersonal presentation from this particular DJ/MC. Don't wait until your wedding day to find out that your DJ isn't qualified to serve as your spokesperson.

◆ What is your entertainment background?

Being a good Master of Ceremonies, fulfilling the role of properly representing you as your spokesperson, will require finding someone with unique talent and skills. Many DJs have limited themselves to DJ training and/or experience alone. Although they may mix music well, their ability to guide, direct, and motivate your guests using announcements that are concise, confident, and effective, may be somewhat limited. However, if they have a wide base of entertainment experience and/or training, their ability to clearly communicate in a polished manner that's fits your expectations may be much more likely. A Talented DJ will have taken classes and/or workshops on acting, singing, public speaking, stand-up comedy, etc. They may even have a background in radio, theater, television, voice over, etc. Be sure to ask your DJ for a description of their entertainment background and allow them to share with you how those experiences have made them a better Master of Ceremonies, spokesperson, and Wedding DJ.

◆ What can you tell me about your services and/or performance that sets you apart from all the rest?

A Talented DJ should be ready to answer this question with gusto. Keep in mind that most DJs do the same things, but it is how they do what they do that truly sets them apart. Most DJs return phone calls. Some do it quickly and some will get back to you in few days. Most DJs will introduce your First Dance. Some will do it in a very personalized way while others might say the same exact thing they have said at every reception for the last 5 years. This question should also be asked of anyone who is recommending you to a particular DJ, whether they are a friend or a wedding vendor. If the DJ says they are the same as all of the rest, but they're just cheaper, this should tell you that they are relying on a low price as their primary attraction. The truth is, if they could do "the same things" in the same way that enables other DJs in their region to charge higher fees, increased demand for their services would enable them to charge just as much if not more as those other DJs.

◆ What improvements have you made in your services and/or performance in the last 2 years?

Maintaining a competitive edge in a performance-based, service industry requires constant, ongoing education and training. It's similar to running up the down escalator…if you stop running…you are losing ground. No performer, whether they are an actor, a musician, or a DJ, ever "arrives" or becomes completed as a performer. The very best DJs continue their education and training via performance workshops, seminars, trade shows and involvement in their local and national trade associations. If the DJ is unable to give you a list of improvements they have made in their services and/or performance, chances are they have become complacent and it's highly likely that they are delivering, at best, an average caliber of services and/or performance. A Talented DJ will be ready to answer this question with confidence because they are always in an ongoing state of improvement. Finally, be sure to ask the DJ if they have attended any national or local trade shows or performance workshops in the last 2 years.

◆ Do you have feedback surveys that will verify your level of skill and talent?

Check their references. Ask for feedback surveys. Take the time to read what their previous clients had to say about their unique skills and talents. If they have feedback surveys, but are not willing to share them with you, perhaps their feedback hasn't been as glowing as they'd like you to believe. Or maybe they are not currently seeking such feedback from their clients. A Talented DJ will be consistently looking for feedback to help them continue to improve their services. Someone who isn't requesting such feedback may be perfectly content with the level of service they are currently providing. However, their clients might not be as content with their services, so be sure to call their references.

◆ Can we come watch you perform at an upcoming wedding reception?

Many of the bridal magazines and books over the years have encouraged brides to request an opportunity to see their prospective DJ in action at a live wedding reception. This advice is not only misguided, it can be downright harmful to the current bride/client as well as the prospective bride/client. When a DJ is performing at a wedding reception, they are "on stage" for at least 4 hours, if not much longer. When a prospective bride/client drops by to watch the DJ in action, she will typically only witness 20 minutes of their total performance. Depending on where they are in the overall agenda, she might only get to see the DJ playing background music during the meal. If the DJ is aware that the prospective bride/client is "dropping by", their focus may become split between fulfilling their current bride/client's agenda and "auditioning" for their prospective bride/client. Strangers should never be allowed to "crash" your own wedding reception, so don't contribute to this problem by crashing someone else's wedding reception when there are already much better ways to verify a DJs skills and talents.

◆ Can we see uncut video footage of you performing at a reception?

Requesting uncut video footage is one of the best ways to verify the true skills and talents of a DJ. They may balk at the idea and suggest that anyone can compile a collection of good video clips while editing out the mistakes. But uncut video footage will show you everything. If they are unwilling to share such footage, perhaps they have something to hide? Talented DJs not only seek feedback via surveys, but they will also often review uncut video footage of their own performances for the purpose of self-critique and personal improvement. When you watch the footage, here are a few things to look for and keep in mind.

Watch the way they make announcements. Is the DJ making announcements in a polished, professional and personalized manner? Listen closely. Do they refer to the bride and groom as "The Bride and Groom" all night long or do they use their names? Do they announce the special dances in a uniquely personalized manner, or does it sound like

"Requesting
uncut
video
footage
is one of
the best ways
to verify
the true skills
and talents
of a DJ."

Auditioning
For
Talent

just about every other wedding announcement you've ever heard? Are they using repetitive phrase like "Ladies and Gentlemen" or "At this time...?" Are they making eye contact with your guests, or do they appear nervous or unsure while they are speaking? Are they rambling endlessly instead of making announcements that are concise and effective? Are they saying anything that you would consider inappropriate? I once heard a story about a Wedding DJ making jokes on the microphone at a reception about his 3 ex-wives. I wrote it off as fiction until I found a real DJ who was bragging online about making such tasteless comments as part of his cake cutting announcements.

Remember, the person you choose will not only be making announcements, but they will also be serving as your spokesperson. Choose the person that you feel will be able to represent you to your guests in the best manner possible.

Watch their transitions. Is the DJ prepared for what comes next after each moment and are they keeping the guests' attention focused? Does the DJ appear unprepared? Is the DJ asking questions on the mic about whether it's time for the next agenda item? Does the DJ have the right music ready for the next moment? Do the various events appear to be flowing smoothly, or are there long pauses between events that are filled with dead air? Keeping your party flowing smoothly requires a skilled entertainer who knows how to direct your events with seamless transitions. Choose the person that you can trust to keep things on track.

Keep in mind that every reception celebration should be crafted uniquely for each couple. Some of the entertaining ideas you see in action on the video may be totally contrary to your personal style and tastes. But, remember that those ideas may have been perfect for that particular couple. Don't let ideas that turn you off cause you to pass on a particular DJ. Look deeper and see if they have the talent and the skill to deliver the kind of entertainment that will be appropriate for you.

◆ How will you create a full dance floor at my reception?

Every DJ should be able to describe their own "Dance Theory" for creating a dance floor filled with guests of all ages and tastes. There are many different ways to create the dancing atmosphere and the right mix of music and interaction needed to turn a group of seated guests into a group of dancing guests. Pay close attention to the answer given by the DJ. If they begin with statements like, "What I always do to get the dancing started is...," or, "What I always play to get the dancing started is...," there is a high likelihood that they have a set play list or a set routine that they deliver the same way at all of their receptions. Some DJs will insist that their use of group dances has always been a sure fire way to kick off the dancing. Some experienced DJs may suggest starting off with older selections that are still popular among all age groups while mixing in the newer music that tends to appeal to your younger guests later in the night. Still others might recommend starting off with a popular romantic slow song to bring up all the couples for a slow dance. Keep in mind…the only responses that are wrong are the ones that will not fit for you and/or your group. Some receptions need a group dance to get things kicked off. Others may turn into a dance party naturally during the course of the meal with no verbal encouragement from the DJ at all. The best answer a Talented DJ could give you to this question might be to respond with a question, such as, "How would you like me to get the dance floor filled?"

◆ Will you and your equipment be presented in an appropriate manner?

One of the most common complaints about DJs at receptions is related to their apparel and the look of their equipment set-ups. Some amateur DJs have been known to show up at a reception in black jeans, sneakers, and a tuxedo print t-shirt. But most Talented DJs recognize that a formal celebration calls for a Master of Ceremonies in formal attire. Granted, some couples may opt for a costumed theme or a casual dress code, but they will also undoubtedly request that their DJ dress to match the occasion. Ask to see photos of the DJ, and/or their staff, at a recent reception. Be clear with your DJ about your dress code expectations.

While you're at it, request to see some photos of their typical equipment set-ups at a recent reception. Are there unsightly cords and wires hanging out in plain sight?(1) If they use lights, do their lights fit with your reception location's décor, or do they look like the kind of lights you'd expect to see at a High School Prom?(2) Keep in mind that the DJ's equipment set-ups may end up in the backdrop of many of the photos taken at your reception. Some DJs have gone so far as to put covers on their speakers and draping, or a façade, in front of their equipment set-ups to make them look more aesthetically pleasing. Bob Carpenter, a popular wedding entertainer in Greenville, RI, is using the new BOSE® L1™ Cylindrical Radiator® System, but can you see them in the photo?(4) Andy Austin, a popular wedding entertainer in Dallas/Forth Worth, TX, actually has a creative façade that can be customized to match the color of the bridesmaid's dresses or the table linens.(5) You'll be investing a lot of time and money creating the colors and décor that will dress up your reception. Make sure your DJ's equipment set-ups will fit into that setting as well.

◆ What is more important, professional equipment or unique talent?

This question is specifically designed to help you identify if the DJ/MC believes their real value is found in the amount and quality of sound equipment they provide, or in their uniquely specialized talents. Many DJs suffer from the misconception that what they bring (their gear) is more important or has more value than what they can do (their talent). This can be plainly seen when visiting their web sites with prominent pictures of their speakers, microphones, light shows, mixers, amps, equipment set-ups. Or best of all...pictures of themselves holding their microphones in front of their speakers and their light shows.(3)

DJ Set-ups: The Good, The Bad, & The Ugly

1: How Many Watts?

2: Pretty Flashy?!

3: We've Got The Tools!

4: BOSE® L1™…Nice!

5: Finely Furnished!

Did your caterer show you photos of their chafing dishes? Did your photographer show you their collection of lenses? When you see photos like these being emphasized over the unique talents and skills that a Talented DJ, or a Wedding Entertainment Director™ will regularly provide, you can be sure that you are dealing with an Average Wedding DJ. This reveals that the DJ believes you should be most concerned with the amount and quality of gear they will bring to your reception. If they have mistakenly focused on their gear instead of their talent, then they might be choosing to buy newer and better equipment instead of investing in techniques and opportunities for improving their talents. But if great gear was all that was required to make yours "The Best Wedding Reception...Ever!", then you could just rent the necessary equipment and have your friends provide your entertainment.

However, if the DJ acknowledges that unique talent is the most important factor in creating an unforgettably fun celebration, then you are probably speaking with a truly Talented DJ or one who is well on their way towards becoming a Talented DJ.

◆ Will you charge us extra for additional speakers and/or cordless microphones?

This would be comparable to your photographer charging you extra to bring a wide angle lens. A Talented DJ will make sure that they have the necessary tools to properly deliver their service and performance. But a DJ who isn't already charging a professional fee to begin with, will be more likely to tack on extra fees for the basic tools they should already have available to get the job done right. However, if you want a large lighting set-up, that often requires more staff to set up and run the additional equipment. So, it would be reasonable to pay extra for such additional equipment services.

◆ What kind of backup systems do you have for your PA equipment?

When you fly as a passenger on a commercial airplane, there are often 2 or 3 different control systems available to the pilots so they will still be able to control the plane, even if 1 or 2 of their redundant systems are lost due to a malfunction in mid-flight. If your DJ has just one CD deck, one computer, one mixer, or one amplifier and any one of these components suffers a malfunction in the middle of your reception, your celebration could take a dramatic turn for the worse. Professional entertainers know from experience that redundant systems are needed to ensure an uninterrupted performance at your reception.

At a recent reception, my DJ mixer began to malfunction during my initial sound-check. I was able to swap out the defective mixer and replace it with a back-up mixer well before any serious problems could have occurred. But if I had not had my back-up mixer on site, my reception performance could have suffered severely. Backup PA equipment is really only a backup if your DJ actually brings it along.

◆ How many microphones will you provide for our wedding ceremony?

This may seem like an unimportant question at first glance, until you experience a wedding ceremony where the minister can be clearly heard, but the bride and groom cannot. The overall purpose of a wedding reception is to celebrate your lifelong commitment of marriage. But if your guests can't hear the two of you exchanging your vows, then they will feel left out in the middle of your ceremony. At a recent ceremony I attended as a guest, the minister was given a lavaliere microphone (a clip-on lapel mic) by the location, but there was no mic provided for the bride and groom. As they began sharing their personally written vows, even their parents in the front row couldn't hear the emotion-filled words they were exchanging. Your words and your voices will be of the utmost importance at that particular moment. Feel free to insist that the DJ provide 2 lavaliere/lapel microphones for your ceremony, or at least a handheld cordless microphone that the minister can use to let your guests hear your vows.

Presenting the Wedding Entertainment Director™

Since the beginning of wedding celebrations, music and entertainment has undoubtedly played a major role in creating fun-filled, memorable moments. Bands were the only option for musical entertainment until Mobile Disc Jockeys came on the scene in the early 1970's. But at the time, most DJs delivered the same service as Bands...they just played music. In an effort to provide more value to their wedding clients while creating more successfully entertaining receptions, some Disc Jockeys began serving as the Master of Ceremonies. Soon, many DJs began promising to offer the same level and quality of services, with little to no training as MCs, for "half the price." The generally accepted idea was that being a DJ was easy and fun and just about anyone could do it with very little time, effort, or money invested.

It became apparent that the term Disc Jockey, when referring to wedding entertainment, had become branded with descriptions like these excerpts from the NPR iPod story: "The guy in the powder blue tux...shouting out dumb jokes and whopping and hollering to the chorus of...'Celebration'...boisterous...cheesy deejay..."[2] This overall negative branding in the public's perception caused some DJs, who were striving to deliver the very best quality in service and performance for their wedding clients, to create a new identity for themselves. Because their services had expanded well beyond just playing music and/or making announcements as the MC, they recognized a valid need to create a new name for their wedding entertainment services. As a result, in early 2001, the new title of Wedding Entertainment Director™ was developed.

The 7 services provided by all Wedding Entertainment Directors™ are: *Comprehensive Personalization, Creative Involvement, Event Direction, Talented Spokesperson, Music Programming, Appropriate Presentation, and Quality Amplification.*

"If your guests can't hear the two of you exchanging your vows, then they will feel left out in the middle of your ceremony."

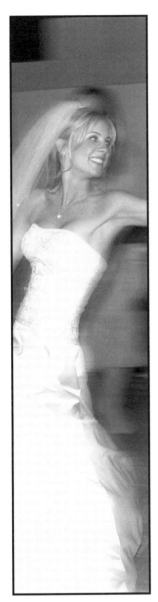

In an effort to ensure that every Wedding Entertainment Director™ will provide each of these services to a measurable, professional caliber, the Wedding Entertainment Directors Guild™ was formed. The Wedding Entertainment Directors Guild™ utilizes a rigorous application process to verify that each and every member is a proven professional with a minimum of 5 years experience in wedding entertainment and/or a minimum of 200 wedding reception performances. To see just how strenuous and thorough the rest of this application process is, feel free to visit the web site for the Wedding Entertainment Directors Guild™ (http://www.wedguild.com)

Once a member has completed their application process and has been approved for membership within the Wedding Entertainment Directors Guild™, they will be able to identify themselves as a true Wedding Entertainment Director™ with this logo:

It should be noted that anyone promoting themselves as a Wedding Entertainment Director™, with or without this logo, should always be verified as such by visiting the membership roster listing at the Wedding Entertainment Directors Guild™ web site (http://www.wedguild.com).

If you are considering hiring a Wedding Entertainment Director™ to provide the entertainment at your wedding reception, here are some important benefits to consider as you prepare to make your decision.

+ Wedding Entertainment Directors™ are proven professionals.
+ Wedding Entertainment Directors™ mix pre-recorded music extremely well.
+ Wedding Entertainment Directors™ have a wide variety of music genres.
+ Wedding Entertainment Directors™ excel in planning and directing receptions so your celebration will flow smoothly.
+ Wedding Entertainment Directors™ are passionate about creating unforgettably fun receptions.

The 7 services that each Wedding Entertainment Director™ regularly provides for their brides and grooms (as listed earlier), are the necessary components for creating a personalized entertainment experience that will not be soon forgotten. Let's take a few moments to explore these services in greater detail.

The Best
Wedding
Reception
...Ever!

◆ What is Comprehensive Personalization?

Comprehensive Personalization includes helping you plan your ceremony and/or reception agenda, with a timeline of events, a list of participants who will be involved or may need to be introduced, and your musical preferences for: the background music, the songs for each special moment, and the requests to be played during open dancing.

Wedding Entertainment Directors™ specialize in helping you to create your ceremony and/or reception agenda from the entertainment perspective. During your initial consultation and planning process, they will listen to your ideas while offering their experienced advice to ensure that your schedule of events will not only be uniquely yours, but it will also be thoroughly entertaining for your family and friends as well. They will help you select the traditional events that fit your style and then organize them into a script that will keep your celebration moving along at a pace of your choosing. They will help you create the lineup order for your wedding party's grand entrance while making sure they can confidently pronounce any difficult names. They will offer you a large variety of musical choices as they seek your input on the 3 categories of musical selections: Background, Special Moments, and Dancing Requests. They will provide you with a list of suggestions for background music, while remaining open to any of your own unique ideas. They will provide you with a list of suggestions for your ceremony processional and recessional music, while encouraging you to add any of your own personal choices. They will provide you with a list of suggestions for sound-tracking the various special moments during your reception (i.e. cake cutting, grand entrance, etc.), while inviting you to weigh in with your own creative selections. They will provide you with a list of suggestions for your dancing requests from a wide variety of genres and eras, while offering you the opportunity to add any of your favorite tunes to their list. They will give you the freedom to create a "do not play" list, so you won't be bothered by songs you severely dislike on your wedding day. When your reception comes to an end, the agenda, the flow, and the musical selections will all have been completely personalized to fit your unique style, taste, and personality.

◆ What is Creative Involvement?

Creative Involvement includes providing you with ideas that are designed to make your guests feel more involved throughout your celebration and may also include the development of ideas that have been custom crafted for your unique situation.

Wedding Entertainment Directors™ have a wide variety of suggestions for creating appropriate guest involvement in a reception environment. These ideas may include, but are not limited to: centerpiece giveaways, sing-along activities, buffet release ideas, creative methods for personalizing your wedding party's grand entrance, etc. These ideas will be explored in greater detail in Part III: "Adding Your Personal Style."

Auditioning
For
Talent

73

Wedding Entertainment Directors™ are also known for helping couples create memorable moments with their guests that are completely unique to a given situation. To see a clear example of how a surprise entrée choice was turned into a moment that involved the guests in a simple, yet entertaining way, turn back to page 19 and read the spotlight segment on Pete & Nichole's Reception.

No one wants to feel left out at a wedding reception. When your guests are allowed, or better yet invited, to become active participants throughout your reception celebration, they will relax, they will make new friends, they will have more fun, they will be more inclined to dance when the time comes, and they will stay longer. A Wedding Entertainment Director™ will be able to advise you about selecting the right amount of involvement for your group so that everyone has an enjoyable time without feeling over-involved as well.

◆ What is Event Direction?

Event Direction is the art and science of keeping your agenda on track while keeping your guests entertained. The science part includes double checking the important details behind the scenes (i.e. Making sure the cake knife is at the cake table.) and communicating with your reception team members (i.e the caterer, the photographer, the videographer, etc.) to make sure everything and everyone is ready before moving onto the next activity on your agenda. The art part includes "reading your crowd" to make sure they are not getting bored or restless while making sure they never see the science part taking place (i.e. Announcing for someone to go find the cake knife over the PA system.).

Wedding Entertainment Directors™ consistently go out of their way to communicate in advance with your ceremony and/or reception team members, including: your ceremony officiate, your wedding coordinator, your caterer, your photographer, and your videographer. They have learned from experience that your team of vendors will work together better and your reception will flow more smoothly when everyone is working off of the same script. If your photographer wants to take a group photo with all of the guests, a Wedding Entertainment Director™ will work with you and your photographer to place the group photo into your agenda where it will do the most good and the least harm.

Wedding Entertainment Directors™ always use a preventative direction checklist to manage the details behind the scenes at your ceremony and/or reception that could turn into possible problems later on. Like a director for a movie or a play, they have come to recognize that each important person and/or prop needs to be in place and ready at the right time for your reception's events to move as smoothly as the action on the screen during an entertaining movie. If the photographer is out of the room, a Wedding Entertainment Director™ will make sure they are aware of the next special event that is about to occur, so they will have plenty of time to return and get ready for their next important photograph. If champagne for the toast has not yet been poured, a Wedding Entertainment Director™ will alert the catering staff and then wait until everyone has been served before beginning the formal toasts. A Wedding Entertainment Director™ will always be more than happy to show you the reception direction checklist they use to keep your celebration moving along smoothly.

Wedding Entertainment Directors™ will always insist on becoming familiar with the setting provided by your chosen location for your ceremony and/or reception. They know how important room layout can be for the overall success of an entertaining reception. If 70% of the guests are seated around the corner from the head table, then the toasts will need to take place in a spot that is easily visible to all of your guests. Extra amplification may also be needed to make sure those toasts can be heard around that corner.

Some of these services may already be provided by your wedding coordinator, so there may be some overlap with the details that are managed by a Wedding Entertainment Director™. This subject will be covered in greater detail in Chapter 8: "Nominating the Best Director." It should be stated, however, that a Wedding Entertainment Director™ will still insist on double-checking the details that can directly impact the pacing and flow of your reception.

◆ How will a Talented Spokesperson make my reception better?

A Talented Spokesperson will utilize their proven skills at public speaking, along with any additional entertainment training and/or experience they may have, to communicate with your guests in a manner that captures their attention, keeps them properly informed, and encourages them to have an enjoyable time.

Wedding Entertainment Directors™ have not only invested a lot of time into improving their abilities as public speakers, but they have also expanded their capabilities as entertainers. Many have a taken a class and/or a workshop on acting, singing, dancing, or even stand-up comedy. Some have even worked in television and/or radio. They have learned from experience that the confidence to speak well in front of a live audience comes from ongoing practice, rehearsal, and training.

Wedding Entertainment Directors™ also recognize that beyond just making announcements, everything they say verbally and non-verbally will reflect directly on you. This fact alone compels them to get to know you on a personal level. Don't be surprised if they want to get to know everything they can about your families, the history of your relationship, your likes and dislikes in both music and humor, what you do for a living, etc. By knowing you well, a Wedding Entertainment Director™ will feel confident to not only speak well, but they will also innately know the right thing to say in the right moment.

◆ What is Music Programming?

Music Programming is the art and science of playing just the right songs in just the right sequence to create a mood, a feeling, a memory, or even a dance floor filled with guests dancing at your reception. The science part includes the following: a wide knowledge of various music genres, confidently knowing the proper use of audio mixing equipment, understanding how the beats per minute in a given song can build or decrease energy, and staying informed about the best songs from every era for creating dancing. The art part includes the following: being able to "read the crowd" and adjust the music accordingly, knowing when to lead the crowd into a different genre or a slow song, having the ability to create a mix of background music that gradually builds energy, and the creativity to build sets of music in a given genre. Suffice it to say, there is no way that an iPod could ever duplicate the art and science that is required to create good music programming. But it should also be pointed out that regardless of how easy or fun it looks, when you see someone doing a great job of music programming, it truly requires some uniquely honed skills and specialized talents to create the right mix of music for the right crowd.

Wedding Entertainment Directors™ are highly skilled at mixing music, whether it's your background selections, the songs you've selected for your special moments, or formatting your dancing requests. The music lists they'll share with you will undoubtedly be just the tip of the iceberg when it comes to the full contents of their total music collections. They have been practicing the art and science of music programming for years to achieve the skill levels they currently posses. But many of them will also tell you that they are still learning and improving their skills, just as it has always been with great actors, singers and the like.

Wedding Entertainment Directors™ have also developed skills, as needed, in the field of audio editing. They have found that sometimes a Father/Daughter Dance song that has been edited to last less than 3 minutes may be preferred by a bride when compared to the original version of the song that lasts over 5 minutes. Or perhaps the bride wants her Father/Daughter Dance song to incorporate a special, pre-recorded dedication to her dad. Being skilled at audio editing allows Wedding Entertainment Directors™ to be able to help their brides and grooms create special moments like these that will be even more meaningful.

Finally, all Wedding Entertainment Directors™ have taken the time to develop their own ideas and methods related to "Dance Theory." There are likely to be a wide variety of working "Dance Theory" models, as there are many different methods and options available for creating good dancing at a wedding reception. A Wedding Entertainment Director™ will be able to confidently share with you the philosophy, methods, and ideas that have shaped their personal "Dance Theory" for creating lots of fun-filled dancing at their receptions.

The Best
Wedding
Reception
...Ever!

◆ What is Appropriate Presentation?

Appropriate Presentation includes making sure that the entertainment (whether it's a Band, a DJ/MC, or a Wedding Entertainment Director™) is dressed in a manner that is fitting for your celebration. If your reception's dress code will be very formal, then a tuxedo may be the best fit. If your reception's dress code is a casual Hawaiian theme, then khakis and a Hawaiian shirt might be better. But this should also include the presentation of the entertainment's PA equipment, control booth, and/or stage area.

Wedding Entertainment Directors™ always take great care to present themselves in a manner that is well-groomed, polished, and professional. They will communicate with you in advance about your reception's dress code to ensure that they do not appear out of place. And they are also very conscientious about ensuring that their PA equipment, control booth and/or stage area are kept neat, clean, and suitable for the setting you've worked so hard to create.

◆ What is Quality Amplification?

Quality Amplification includes providing any and all professional grade PA support equipment necessary to ensure that your guests will not miss a single important announcement, formal toast, or even your vows during your ceremony. This will also include being able to create enough volume for the dancing near the dance floor, while also being able to maintain levels that allow for comfortable conversation during the meal. Wedding Entertainment Directors™ take great pride in delivering the best quality sound for their brides and grooms. They always bring at least 2 lavaliere microphones (clip-on lapel mics) for wedding ceremonies so your guests will be able to listen in as you share your vows. They can provide PA support for your cocktail hour, even if it is set in a separate location from your ceremony and/or reception. They will have a cordless microphone available for your formal toasts. They can handle additional sound support needs if the size of your group requires it. The bottom line is…Wedding Entertainment Directors™ always bring the proper tools to make sure things are done right.

Conclusion

Whether your choices will include finding a Minister/Officiate, using your iPod, choosing a Band, booking a DJ/MC, or securing a Wedding Entertainment Director™, seek out the best wedding entertainment you can find by asking the right questions and taking the time to meet with them in person. Choose someone who has the talents that you find appealing, the skills to turn your dreams into reality, and the personality to entertain your guests in a style and manner that will fulfill and exceed your expectations. Not only will your guests enjoy themselves more as a result, but they will also be raving for months and years to come that yours was "The Best Wedding Reception...Ever!"

CHAPTER 8

NOMINATING THE BEST DIRECTOR
Appointing the Best Person to Guide and Direct Your Reception

When a movie receives rave reviews from the critics and public alike, the success of the film is usually attributed to the artistic vision and efforts of the director. The director often re-works the script to make sure the dialogue and scenes will flow naturally. The director also makes sure the various props are in place and the actors know their blocking and their cues. Finally, the director oversees the filming of each scene to make sure the proper actions and emotions have been created and captured in a manner that keeps the overall plot moving along effectively. Good entertainment always requires someone to fulfill the role of the director, whether the entertainment in question is an exciting, fast-paced movie or an unforgettably fun wedding reception. But far too often at wedding receptions, these duties are overlooked or they are taken on by someone who may not be qualified to create a unique entertainment experience. This chapter will be helpful in clarifying who you should trust to serve as the director of your celebration.

A Good Director Always Has a Plan

An entertaining wedding reception won't just fall into place all by itself. Whomever you choose as your director should be able to help you create an agenda that will not only incorporate your personal style, but will also maintain the proper pacing and flow required to keep your guests interested and involved. If the director of a movie can tell that the script is too slow or too wordy, the director will make changes to speed up the dialogue to more succinctly communicate the point of a given scene. In a similar manner, the director of your reception will offer advice and suggestions to ensure that your chosen formalities are scheduled into your agenda in the most effective way possible. This subject will be covered in greater detail in Part II: "Creating Your Timeline."

The methods for creating your agenda may differ from director to director, however it is vital that you include your entertainment vendor in this process. Some locations may prefer to have someone on their staff serve as your director. But more often than not, the agenda that is created by the location will be one that best suits the needs of their staff or the personal preferences of the location's owner, rather than being designed to create a smooth-flowing entertainment experience. Some wedding coordinators may prefer to create your agenda timeline without any input from your entertainment vendors. If their experience includes creating

receptions that have been highly entertaining, not just well decorated, then their input on your agenda may be all you need. However, if their strengths are more focused on the décor rather than keeping your guests engaged in your celebration, you may be allowing a "producer" to serve as your "director" and the results could be very disappointing. Some DJs and Bands will work with you to create an agenda that will not only be fun, but will also keep your reception events moving along with very little downtime. A Wedding Entertainment Director™ will insist on meeting with you in advance to create an agenda that will result in a smooth-flowing, personalized reception agenda.

In a recent phone conversation with a professional wedding coordinator, I was told point blank that being present at an agenda planning meeting was "not my place." It was made very clear to me by this coordinator that my role was to plan the music choices only, and she would inform me about the reception agenda 2 weeks prior to the wedding date. If my role was to "just play the music" then I would be in agreement with her. But as the MC and Wedding Entertainment Director™, I had a vital role to play in ensuring that my client's reception celebration would be as fun as possible. It became apparent that we were at an impasse.

The input your entertainment vendors have to offer regarding your agenda should be given a high priority, if not top priority. They are the ones who will have to make your party work. But if they are forced to use a script that isn't entertaining, or may be wrought with downtime, then their job will not only be much more difficult, but the quality of the results they will be able to deliver (guests enjoying themselves, more guests dancing, etc.) may be hampered as well. Your location staff wouldn't dream of telling your photographer not to use their flash to capture your special moments. Your coordinator would never tell your cake maker to leave off the frosting. Yet it is all too common to find locations and coordinators who will tell your entertainment vendors to carry out an agenda that may have serious flaws.

If creating an entertaining reception celebration is high on your list of priorities, then it is imperative that whomever you select to serve as your director should be someone who is highly qualified to create an agenda that will not only flow smoothly, but also be thoroughly entertaining.

Directing a Reception Requires Entertainment Experience

There is a good reason why many movie actors have been able to transition successfully into becoming movie directors. Due to their experience in creating entertaining moments in front of the camera, they realized that they had a well-developed skill set for creating such moments from behind the camera as well. It should also be noted that the best directors are known not only for their innovative ideas, but also for creating movies that were powerfully emotional, incredibly memorable, and captivatingly entertaining. Likewise, the director you choose may help you create an emotional, memorable, and entertaining reception.

A director's primary role is to create a movie, a stage play, or a wedding reception that will be creative and consistently entertaining. For this reason alone, it makes very little sense to hand over these duties to someone who doesn't have either entertainment experience or a deep understanding about creating effectively entertaining moments.

If you have ever been a guest at a wedding reception that just dragged along with no idea what would be happening next, chances are that no one was selected to serve as the director, or whoever was entrusted with the director's duties lacked the entertainment experience and knowledge to keep the reception agenda moving at a steady pace.

Often, the best way to clarify the roles that will be fulfilled by the vendors you will be entrusting to guide your reception, is to explore the definition of the terms and titles carried by each.

◆ *Coordinator*
Somebody bringing together different elements: somebody responsible for organizing diverse parts of an enterprise or groups into a coherent or efficient whole.[1]

◆ *Producer*
A person responsible for the financial and administrative aspects of a stage, film, television, or radio production; the person who exercises general supervision of a production and is responsible chiefly for raising money, hiring technicians and artists, etc., required to stage a play, make a motion picture, or the like.[2]

◆ *Master Of Ceremonies*
A person who directs the entertainment at a party, dinner, nightclub, radio or television broadcast, or the like, acting as host and introducing the speakers or performers.[3]

◆ *Director*
The person responsible for the interpretive aspects of a stage, film, or television production; the person who supervises the integration of all the elements, as acting, staging, and lighting, required to realize the writer's conception.[4]

It should be noted that the definitions for Coordinator and Producer are very similar in description, scope and responsibilities. There are also striking differences between the clearly defined roles of a Producer and a Director. Finally, it is also quite remarkable that the definition given for Master of Ceremonies utilizes the phrase "directs the entertainment" in describing the duties and services provided.

Unfortunately, many entertainers who are chosen to fulfill the role as the Master of Ceremonies are commonly unprepared to actually direct the pacing and flow of their wedding receptions. Similarly, most Wedding Coordinators have only been trained to function as producers and are lacking in the entertainment experience needed to effectively direct the pacing and flow of their events as well. As always, there will be exceptions in both cases. There are some Wedding Coordinators who are quite adept at serving as both the producer and director of their wedding receptions. There are also some entertainers that are quite skilled at directing their events as well. But clearly, based on the definitions alone, the role of the director is one that is focused on the overall entertainment value of the entire function.

These conclusions clearly indicate that the best director for the overall pacing and flow of your reception should be the person who has the most entertainment experience. That person may possibly be your Wedding Coordinator or they may be the person you have selected to serve as your Master of Ceremonies. However, if both have strong entertainment backgrounds, it would be best to nominate your Master of Ceremonies to serve as the director of your reception's overall pacing and flow.

If your Wedding Coordinator recognizes that your Master of Ceremonies has well established skills and talents, they should both be able to work together as a team to ensure that your reception is entirely successful. However, if your Wedding Coordinator is more concerned with being "in charge" of your Master of Ceremonies, unnecessary power struggles could result in mishaps.

A Director is Prepared to Prevent Problems from Occurring

On the set of a movie, the director has taken precautions to make sure the lighting and audio settings are perfect before attempting to film a given scene. In a similar manner, the director at your reception will take precautions to make sure your vendors are ready and in place before starting your First Dance. There are many details that can be overlooked in the process of guiding a reception celebration. Many of these details when missed can cause delays, confusion or even embarrassment.

I have heard stories of DJs announcing the First Dance when the bride and groom were not even in the room. Or the Master of Ceremonies who announced the Cake Cutting without notifying the photographer first. Or the Band leader who introduced the formal toasts before the catering staff had been able to begin serving the champagne. Each of these examples could have been prevented by a qualified director who is using a direction checklist to ensure that the other vendors, the guests of honor, and the necessary props were all set in their proper places before beginning the next scheduled event on the agenda.

Whether your Wedding Coordinator or your Master of Ceremonies will be entrusted with directing your reception, be sure to ask them for a copy of their reception direction checklist. If they are unable to share one with you, perhaps they will just be "winging it" as your reception director. A highly qualified reception director will gladly show you the list of details they manage behind the scenes to prevent problems from occurring.

"the best director for the overall pacing and flow of your reception should be the person who has the most entertainment experience"

The Value of Using a Wedding Entertainment Director™

The best reasons for nominating a Wedding Entertainment Director™ to serve as the director of your reception are contained in the three words used to describe their overall services.

The use of the word "Wedding" clearly communicates that a Wedding Entertainment Director™ is someone who truly specializes in weddings. Directing corporate functions or a birthday party celebration or even a school dance can require entirely different skill sets. Someone who has a deep understanding of the etiquette, traditions, and personalization that can be required to create a truly unforgettable reception celebration will always treat each wedding reception with their very best personal service. Whereas a director who "specializes" (and I use that term loosely) in a wide variety of events may be more inclined to treat their wedding receptions as just another "gig."

The use of the word "Entertainment" clearly communicates that a Wedding Entertainment Director™ is someone who is an experienced and talented entertainer. They will know exactly how to make your wedding reception as entertaining as possible. Whereas a director whose focus and background encompasses producing the overall décor may be able to create a visually stimulating setting, while the pacing, flow and total entertainment experience may still come up short.

The use of the word "Director" clearly communicates that a Wedding Entertainment Director™ is someone who not only knows how to direct an entertaining reception, but has proven that their skill levels as a director are truly professional. Some who claim to direct their receptions are merely solving problems after they occur, instead of preventing them from ever becoming problems in the first place. Some of them will "direct" your special moments by interrupting them or even talking over them on their microphone. But a Wedding Entertainment Director™ will always strive to do most of their directing from behind the scenes.

Conclusion

If you want your reception to be a fun, smooth-flowing, and entertaining celebration, then it is vital that you select someone who is well qualified to serve as the director. This decision, more than any other, can have the greatest impact on whether your guests get bored and restless, or whether they enjoy themselves so much that they'll find themselves commenting that yours was truly "The Best Wedding Reception…Ever!"

PART II

CREATING YOUR TIMELINE
Writing a Reception Plan That Will Flow Smoothly

Great entertainment cannot happen without a great script. Too often the fun moments of a wedding reception can become just "to do" items on a checklist. However, if your definition of a successful reception calls for the fun moments to be the focus and the priority, this section will help you to create a timeline that will flow smoothly while keeping your guests consistently entertained.

CHAPTER 9

PICKING THE PACE
Determining Whether Your Schedule Will be Rushed or Relaxed

Some wedding receptions can feel hurried and even frantic, while others may feel like they'll never end. There are many factors to consider when choosing the pacing for your reception. Your personal preferences about pacing might be thwarted by your location's time constraints, your guest count, or even your photographer's schedule. This chapter will help you to determine what kind of pacing will fit best for your celebration. We will also examine some of the common roadblocks that could complicate the pacing you are hoping to achieve.

The Relaxed Reception Schedule

When describing a relaxed reception schedule, these are some of the images that come to mind: A formal, elegant reception with a 5 course meal that is served over 2 hours. A large celebration with food stations that will remain open for most of the evening. An extended cocktail hour with tray-passed hors d'oeuvres followed by a reception filled with more dancing and less of the traditional festivities. Guests who have plenty of time to connect with and congratulate the Bride and Groom.

These images all evoke feelings of a fun celebration that was laid back and stress-free. Such a relaxed schedule could take place over 4 to 8 hours or even longer. If creating this relaxed pace is desired with a time frame that is limited to only 4 hours, then combining or cutting some of the traditional festivities may be necessary. However, with a longer time frame, creating such a relaxed schedule will not only be much easier to achieve, but there will also be less pressure to combine or cut any of the traditional festivities.

There are also some drawbacks to keep in mind when considering the relaxed reception schedule. If your schedule becomes too relaxed, the possibility of your guests getting bored or restless may increase. If your reception director is not adept at "reading the crowd" to see the onset of boredom before it occurs, they may stick with the current plan instead of taking steps to pick up the pace when and if it may be needed. If your Master of Ceremonies is not prepared to properly keep your guests informed about what may be coming up next and when the events will be occurring, they could begin to feel "left out" of your celebration. These kinds of feelings can quickly lead many of your guests to begin thinking about leaving sooner than you might have originally wanted.

The Rushed Reception Schedule

When describing a rushed reception schedule, these are some of the images that come to mind: A fun, energetic reception where something new is always happening from one minute to the next. The dancing starts early and ends early, while you still have a large crowd on the dance floor. Perhaps the guests will enjoy a quick buffet dinner or just heavy appetizers and a chocolate fountain. A celebration that starts off fun, stays fun, and ends on a high note.

These images all evoke feelings of a lively celebration that is fast-paced. Such a rushed schedule could take place over 4 to 5 hours, but probably shouldn't last much longer than that. Some of the traditional festivities may need to be cut and/or combined, especially if having more time for dancing is a high priority.

There are also some drawbacks to keep in mind when considering the rushed reception schedule. If your schedule becomes too rushed, your guests could easily begin to feel overwhelmed and even worn out. If your reception director is accustomed to a more relaxed schedule, then their ability to prevent problems from occurring might be diminished due to the faster pacing of your events. Your Master of Ceremonies may mistakenly become too energetic, too quickly, in an effort to get your guests involved. An overeager MC could easily become a "turn off" for your guests.

The Blended Reception Schedule

A blended reception schedule takes the best aspects of both previous examples and combines them into a schedule that may start off relaxed while slowly building into a celebration that becomes highly energetic. Imagine your guests enjoying a laid back cocktail hour and then, as the reception begins, the pacing rises along a growing energy curve that will culminate in a fully packed dance floor with everyone feeling involved.

The blended reception schedule can work for a 4 hour reception as well as a celebration that lasts 8 hours or longer. If your schedule will only be 4 or 5 hours long, you may still need to consider cutting and/or combining some of the traditional festivities. Especially if having more time for open dancing is a high priority.

There are also some drawbacks to considering the blended reception schedule. If your schedule builds energy too slowly, guests could bore more quickly. If your schedule builds energy too quickly, your guests may get worn out too soon, especially if your time frame is longer than 6 hours. If your reception director is not familiar with creating an energy curve that builds, they may find this pacing difficult to mange effectively. If your Master of Ceremonies is too subdued for too long, the energy might not build when needed. If your Master of Ceremonies is too energetic too early, your guests may get "turned off."

Possible Location Time Constraints

If your location only allows a 4 to 5 hour time frame for your ceremony and/or reception schedule, then creating a relaxed reception schedule may be a bit more challenging. However, if your location will give you an unlimited time frame (8 hours or more), you should be free to create just about any kind of pacing you'd like for your reception.

Some locations have time constraints because they schedule more than one event/reception per day. Others may have time constraints due to local ordinances concerning noise levels late at night. And finally, some places may have limitations on how late they can serve alcohol.

As I already discussed in great detail in Chapter 4: "Scouting for the Perfect Location", determining what the time constraints are should play an important role in helping you select the right location for your needs.

Some venues will host your ceremony, cocktail hour, and reception, but the room for your reception may only be ready at a set time, due to cleanup constraints from whatever was scheduled to take place in that room previously. This information is important to know because your ceremony, cocktail hour, and reception may be scheduled to take place at the entire facility from 5:00pm to 11:00pm, but if the reception room itself will not be ready until 7:00pm, then you will only have 4 hours to complete your traditional festivities, the meal, and the dancing. Such limitations could understandably have a dramatic impact on the desired pacing for your reception celebration.

It's also important to ask not only how long your reception can last, but also what their required cut off time is for the music and dancing. Some locations will tell you that you have until 11:00pm, when in fact, that is the deadline by which all of your guests need to be gone, and your personal clean up completed. For facilities that have such a deadline, some may require that the music and dancing end no later than 10:30pm. If information like this is not discussed in advance, it can create some real frustrations. Especially if you and your guests may have been hoping to dance a little longer, and the celebration is forced to stop much sooner than you had been expecting.

Guest Count Considerations

The number of guests you are inviting can have an undeniable impact on the pacing for your reception celebration. If you want a rushed reception schedule, but you have over 300 guests in attendance, it will become very cumbersome to move quickly from one event to the next. Delays can be caused simply by the difficulty created in locating your other vendors and any VIPs that are needed in the large crowd before beginning the next event on your agenda. When determining what kind of pacing will fit best for your reception, don't overlook the affect your guest count can have on your plans.

Working with Your Other Vendors' Schedules

The time you have scheduled with your other vendors can also have an impact on the overall pacing of your reception. If your reception will last until 11:00pm, but you only have your photographer contracted until 9:00pm, then you may have to rush through some of your festivities a little faster than desired to ensure that those moments are captured before your photographer will be leaving. If you and your photographer have discussed going outdoors for sunset photos, your absence could have a dramatic effect on the pacing of your reception, depending on how your agenda has been scheduled out.

Whenever possible, it is highly recommended to secure vendors who will be present for your entire celebration from the beginning until the end. The pressure caused by making changes to your reception's schedule to accommodate a vendor whose time is almost up can cause big problems for the desired pacing you were hoping to achieve.

You should also make sure you are fully aware of how much your other vendors, including your entertainment, will expect to be paid for going "overtime" past their contractual obligations. Some vendors may give you a price break on added hours when you first book with them, but then charge much more for added hours if they are tacked on at the event itself. If you are aware that it will cost you more to wait until the reception to decide on extending their services, just make sure you are clear in advance how much more it will cost you. Some vendors offer unlimited time as part of their services.

Be Prepared to Make Changes if Needed

If the pacing you have designed is not working for whatever reason, it may be wise to remain open to the idea of making changes in your pacing to ensure that your guests will continue to have an enjoyable time at your reception. This subject will be covered in greater detail in Chapter 12: "Preparing a 'Plan B'."

If the pacing of your reception is more important to you than the overall experience of your guests enjoying themselves, then stick to the pacing plan you have designed. But if creating lasting memories of a fun celebration for your guests is your highest priority, then stay ready to make any changes that may be needed to pick up the pace or even slow it down to create a better overall celebration.

Conclusion

The pacing for your reception is completely your choice. There are many factors covered in this chapter that may limit or even constrain what may be possible, but hopefully you will be able to create the pacing that will not only fit your style and desires, but will also result in a celebration that is uniquely entertaining as well.

"it may be wise to remain open to the idea of making changes in your pacing to ensure that your guests will continue to have an enjoyable time"

JEFF & VICTORIA

May 30th, 2004
Newport Beach, California

RECEPTION AGENDA

4:00-4:40
Drinks & Appetizers
4:40
Grand Entrance
"California"
by Phantom Planet
4:50
Toasts
5:00-7:00
5 Course Dinner
5:00
1st Course-Appetizer
5:10
First Dance
"Your Song"
by Ewan McGregor
5:15
Parents Dance
"Wonderful Tonight"
by Eric Clapton
5:20
2nd Course-Soup
5:30
Longevity Spotlight
5:45
3rd Course-Salad
6:00
Jeff & Victoria's Toast
6:10
4th Course-Entrée
6:35
Bouquet Presentation*
6:40
5th Course-Dessert
6:50
RSVP Spotlight
7:00
Cake Cutting
"Grow Old With You"
by Adam Sandler
"When I'm Sixty-Four"
by The Beatles
7:15-8:25
Open Dancing
8:25
Last Dance
"The Last Dance"
by Frank Sinatra

Every Guest was Personally Included

Jeff & Victoria wanted to create a swanky, classy reception that would still be fun and relaxing for their intimate group of friends and family. The went out of their way to make sure each and every person felt included in a personal way via special dedications and creative interactions that were designed to both entertain and spotlight the individuals who had all played important roles in their lives.

*Bouquet Presentation

As the Bouquet Toss tradition goes, the young lady who catches the Bride's bouquet will supposedly be the next in line to get married. In the spirit of this tradition, Victoria wanted to do something a little more personal. So instead of tossing her bouquet, Victoria chose to present it to her friend, Nancy, who was already engaged to be married.

JEFF & VICTORIA

CHAPTER 10

CHOOSING THE EVENTS
Deciding Which Formalities Will Fit for Your Celebration

Some wedding receptions are very traditional with all of the typical events and festivities that have been commonly done for decades or even for centuries. Others have been crafted with very few or none of the traditional activities, sometimes incorporating new ideas for creating memorable moments. There is no wrong or right any more when it comes to choosing the traditions and activities that that will become a part of your celebration. In this chapter, we will discuss the options for both traditional and modern events, while encouraging you to follow your heart and select the ones that are truly important to you.

The Traditional Events

These are the events that probably took place when your parents got married and maybe even when their parents got married. These events may include: the Cocktail Hour, the Grand Entrance, the Formal Toasts, a Blessing for the Meal, the Meal, the First Dance, the Father/Daughter Dance, the Mother/Son Dance, the Parents Dance, the Wedding Party Dance, the Cake Cutting, the Money Dance/Dollar Dance, the Bouquet Toss, the Garter Removal & Toss, the Last Dance, and the Big Sendoff. See Part III: "Adding Your Personal Style," to see more detailed descriptions of these events.

Some of these traditions may appeal to you, and some others may not. Some of them may feel like requirements. You may feel pressured by certain family members to do one or more of them even though you personally don't care for them. Here is a list of questions to help you in selecting which ones will work for you and which you'd prefer not to do:

◆ Will you have a Cocktail Hour?

If so, you will need to think about whether or not appetizers and drinks will be provided for your guests. If music will be an option, then you will need to think about your preferences in background selections as well.

◆ Will you have a Grand Entrance?

If so, then you will need to think about who will be introduced, in what order and by whom? Will your parents be introduced? How about the ushers or your wedding party? Will there be music? Which selections will create the effect you want to create? Who will your Master of Ceremonies be introducing and will the names be pronounced properly?

◆ Will you have any Formal Toasts?

If so, will it be given by the Best Man, the Father of the Bride, or both? Will anyone else be expected to give a Toast? Will they be told in advance so they can be prepared? Will a cordless, handheld microphone be provided so everyone can hear the toasts? In what order will the Toasts be given? Will the Best Man go first? Will the Groom speak last?

◆ Will someone be asked to give a Blessing for the Meal?

Depending on your religious background and that of your family, this may or may not be something that you want to do. If so, who will you choose to give the Blessing for the Meal? Will they be told in advance so they can be prepared? Will a cordless, handheld microphone be provided so everyone can hear them? Will the catering staff know to wait before serving the meal or opening the buffet or food stations?

◆ Will you provide a Meal?

If so, will it be formal sit-down meal, or a buffet? If it will be a sit down meal, how many courses will be served? Will there be dancing between the courses? If it will be a buffet, will it feature one or more lines? Will there be various food stations? How long will it take the catering staff to serve all of your guests?

◆ Will the two of you have a First Dance?

If so, have you selected a song? Will you be slow dancing or will you be practicing a choreographed dance? Will the song be known to both of you, or will one of you be surprising the other with the selection? When would you like to do your First Dance? If the song feels too long, would you like it to fade out early, or perhaps create a shorter, edited version?

◆ Will the Bride share a special dance with her Father?

If so, have you selected a song? Will you be slow dancing or will you be practicing a choreographed dance? Will the song be known to both of you, or will one of you be surprising the other with the selection? When would you like to do your Father/Daughter Dance? If the song feels too long, would you like it to fade out early, or perhaps create a shorter, edited version?

◆ Will the Groom share a special dance with his Mother?

If so, have you selected a song? Will you be slow dancing or will you be practicing a choreographed dance? Will the song be known to both of you, or will one of you be surprising the other with the selection? When would you like to do your Mother/Son Dance? If the song feels too long, would you like it to fade out early, or perhaps create a shorter, edited version?

◆ Will the two of you share in a special dance with your Parents?

If so, have you selected a song? Will the song be known in advance to all involved, or will they (or you) be surprising the other with the selection? When would you like to do your Parents Dance? Will each of the parents be present and already have a dancing partner?

◆ Will you share a special dance with your Wedding Party?

If so, have you selected a song? Will this be a slow dance or a fast dance? Do you want your Wedding Party members to dance as couples, or can they dance with their spouses and/or dates? When would you like to do your Wedding Party Dance?

◆ Will you have a Cake Cutting?

If so, will you be providing your own cake knife and server? Will you be providing your own cake topper? When would you like to cut your cake? Is there any music selections you'd like played during the Cake Cutting? Do you want your guests to be invited to gather round and take pictures? Will you be feeding each other nicely, or will you be smashing cake? Will there be charms in the cake? Will there also be a Groom's Cake? Who will portion and serve the cake?

◆ Will you have a Money Dance/Dollar Dance?

If so, will both of you be participating? Do you have a purse for the Money Dance? When would you like to do the Money Dance/Dollar Dance? Will your Best Man and Maid of Honor assist you by regulating the lines? Will you be dancing to slow, moderate, or fast songs?

◆ Will you have a Bouquet Toss?

If so, what music selections would you like during your Bouquet Toss? Will your florist be providing a "throw bouquet" for your Bouquet Toss? When would you like to do your Bouquet Toss? How many single ladies will be ready and willing to participate?

◆ Will you be have a Garter Removal & Toss?

If so, what music selections would you like during your Garter Removal & Toss? When would you like to do your Garter Removal & Toss? How many single men will be ready and willing to participate?

◆ Will you be have a Last Dance?

If so, have you selected a song? Will you choose a slow song or a fast song? Will the song be known to both of you, or will one of you be surprising the other with the selection? When would you like to do your Last Dance? Will your guests be asked to share the Last Dance with you?

◆ Will you have a Big Sendoff?

If so, will your guests need any special instructions for participating in your Big Sendoff? Will you be providing your guests with birdseed, flower petals, sparklers, etc.?

The Modern Events

These are the events that have become common or even popular within the last 50 years. These may include: Centerpiece Give-Away Activities, the Video Montage/Slideshow, the Longevity Spotlight, or a Sorority Song. Additional modern events and creative ideas will be covered in greater detail in Part III: "Adding Your Personal Style."

Some of these traditions may appeal to you, and some others may not. Here is a list of questions to help you in selecting which ones will work for you and which ones you'd rather not do:

◆ Will you do any Centerpiece Give-Away Activities?

If so, will the entire centerpiece be okay to take home, or just the floral arrangement itself? Do you want the give-away activity to build energy, or would you prefer to keep things low key? When would you like to do the Centerpiece Give-Away Activity? Will any special props be needed for the activity?

◆ Will you have a Video Montage/Slideshow?

If so, how long will the entire presentation last? Who will be producing the Video Montage/Slideshow? Will there be an audio track included with the Video Montage/Slideshow? Will the proper connections be available to patch the audio feed into the entertainment's sound system? Who will be providing the projector, power extension cables and/or screen for the Video Montage/Slideshow? Where will it all be set up? When would you like to do the Video Montage/Slideshow? Will there be time to test it fully before your Reception begins?

◆ Will you have a Longevity/Anniversary Spotlight?

If so, is there a particular couple, married for a considerable amount of time that you want to spotlight? How many married couples will be present and willing to participate? Do you want to spotlight these married couples at their tables or during a special dance? If this will be during a dance, do you have a song selected? When would you like to do the Longevity/Anniversary Spotlight?

◆ Will you have a Sorority Song?

If so, how many Sorority Sisters will be present and willing to participate? When would you like do the Sorority Song?

Combining Some Events Can Help Conserve Time

If your time frame for your reception celebration will be limited, or if you just want to create some extra time for open dancing, then combining some of your special events may be a helpful solution. Common examples include: combining your First Dance with the Grand Entrance, combining the Father/Daughter Dance and Mother/Son Dance, or combining the Parents and Wedding Party Dances.

Here are some questions to help you determine if combining some events might be a good fit for you:

◆ Would you like to combine your First Dance and Grand Entrance?

If you are from the East Coast, this might not even be an option. We'll cover regional differences in agendas in greater detail in Chapter 11: "Scheduling for Success." Would you like to get your First Dance out of the way as soon as possible, or would you prefer to wait until after the meal? Will the dance floor be cleared for dancing when you make your Grand Entrance, or will it be occupied by the buffet, or your cake table?

◆ Will you combine the Father/Daughter and Mother/Son Dances?

If so, have you selected a song that is more moderate and less focused on either the Bride's Father or the Groom's Mother? Will you both begin at the same time, or will the Bride and her Father go first, while the Groom joins in with his Mother half way through? When would you like to do the Father/Daughter-Mother/Son Dance?

◆ Will you combine the Parents and Wedding Party Dances?

If so, have you selected a song that is more moderate and less focused on either the Parents or the Wedding Party? Will everyone join in together from the beginning, or will you both begin with your Parents and then invite the Wedding Party to join in half way through? Will this be a slow dance or a fast dance? Do you want your Wedding Party members to dance as couples, or can they dance with their spouses and/or dates? When would you like to do the Parents & Wedding Party Dance?

Conclusion

There are lots of questions to consider when choosing the events that will define your reception celebration. Just because some of them may be "traditional" and you may even feel that they are expected, keep in mind that this is your wedding reception. You should do everything that you'd like to do on that day, and nothing that you wouldn't. Don't be afraid to say "No." Likewise, don't be afraid to get creative and come up a completely new idea. I will be discussing each of these issues in greater detail, including creative ways they can be personalized in Part III: "Adding Your Personal Style."

CHAPTER 11

SCHEDULING FOR SUCCESS
Drafting a Script That Will Keep Your Guests Entertained

One of the most common reasons why some wedding receptions feel like things are just dragging along can be attributed to the agenda that maps out the order for the various events. If the script for your celebration is not designed with the overall entertainment value in mind, what may have initially looked like lots of fun on paper, could wind up delivering a rather dull experience instead. In this chapter, we will explore the art and sciences for creating a reception agenda that will keep your guests thoroughly involved and entertained.

Putting Your Desired Pacing Together with Your Events

Now that you have examined the kind of pacing you would like to create for your reception, along with the events that you want to incorporate into your celebration, it's time to put the pieces all together into a format that is both well structured and smooth-flowing. If your desired pacing is rushed, then your events may need to be scheduled closer together with very little downtime between them. If your desired pacing is more relaxed, then you might want to spread some of your events out and give yourself more time to just meet and greet with your guests or even dance. If you want the pacing to start off relaxed, while slowly building into an energetic party, then you may want to put some of the lower energy events early in your schedule while saving some of the higher energy events until later on.

Regional Differences in Agendas Need to be Considered

When planning out your agenda, you should seriously examine the agendas that are the most common to your particular region before determining what order of events will work best for your celebration. One reason why it is so important is that people in different regions have different expectations as to how a reception will flow. If you create an agenda that is completely unfamiliar in your area, your guests will be much more likely to feel like things are not going smoothly. This doesn't mean you have no choice in the matter or that it is impossible to try something new, it's just wise to be aware of the norms before attempting to create something that is drastically different. When your guests hear music that is unfamiliar to them, they may be more inclined to leave the dance floor. In the same way, a reception agenda that is completely unfamiliar in your region could cause some of your guests to assume that your celebration is going badly, even if that truly is not the case.

In New Jersey, the guests will expect to begin dancing right after the grand entrance and then they will continue dancing between each of the meal courses, sitting only when each course is served. While in Southern California, the guests will expect to begin dancing only after the meal has been completely served and cleared. In parts of Wisconsin, the bride and groom will commonly enter their reception with little or no fanfare and then cut their cake without the guests even noticing before being seated at their head table to prepare for the meal. In Sacramento, the bride and groom, along with their wedding party, usually make a big splash with their grand entrance when they first arrive at the reception. And, the cake is commonly cut right at the end of the meal.

As you can clearly see from the examples above, the difference between agendas in various regions can be quite dramatic. As you read through the rest of this book, you will notice several pages that spotlight couples along with their personalized reception agendas. Many of their agendas are quite unique and they might give you some creative ideas for your own reception script.

Don't Overload Your Guests

One common mistake that is made when couples are trying to ensure that their reception will be fun is packing too many events into their agenda in an effort to make sure their guests will never have a chance to get bored. This can result in an agenda that is top heavy with activities, leaving your guests feeling overwhelmed. Too much of a good thing is still too much. More isn't always better. As you read through the creative ideas that will be spelled out later in Part III: "Adding Your Personal Style," don't forget to hold onto only the best ideas, instead of all of the good ideas. Your Master of Ceremonies should also be more than willing to advise you about whether your agenda is becoming too full or not.

Be Discerning With Your Location's Suggested Agenda

Most locations have a pretty good idea about the kinds of agendas that have worked out well in their experiences. But some locations can get downright pushy about your order of events and may even try to require that you follow their suggested timeline, even if it is not an optimal schedule for creating an entertaining reception. These types of locations are, thankfully, rather rare. But, if you are not aware that they will assert more control over the order of your events than you'd prefer before you sign their contract, you may find yourself in a few unpleasant confrontations. If the location does a large number of events, they may have developed certain patterns for their reception agendas that work best for them and their staff. But these preferred patterns may not take into consideration whether the guests will be consistently entertained or will feel bored and restless. I once saw a catering manager turn up the house lights an hour before the dancing was scheduled to finish, so the guests would begin leaving, causing the reception to end prematurely. Sadly, cleaning up early was more important than hosting a celebration.

Some Thoughts on Scheduling the Order of Your Events

Typically, a wedding reception will begin with a Cocktail Hour as the guests are arriving at the location, or are just waiting for the Bride and Groom to finish up with formal photos. When the Wedding Party arrives, there may be a Grand Entrance which may be followed by Formal Toasts, or the First Dance, or even just the Meal itself. Sometimes it may be best to even move to the Cake Cutting right after the Grand Entrance.

At a reception in June of 2006, the bride was following her Vietnamese traditions by changing her dress for a traditional toasting that is done at each table during the meal. Then, after the meal, she changed back into her formal bridal gown. With the limited festivities they had selected and the dress changes factored in, we decided to do their Grand Entrance, followed by the First Dance and then the Cake Cutting, which then led into their Formal Toasts.

The Formal Toasts can be done before the Meal, after the Meal or even before the Cake Cutting. Whichever time you choose for your Formal Toasts, keep your regional expectations in mind and also think about setting it at a time when you will have most, if not all, of your guest's undivided attention.

If you will be asking someone to say a Blessing for the Meal, they will need to be prepared to immediately follow the Formal Toasts if you choose to schedule them before the Meal.

In some regions, the Meal is usually a Buffet with an informal receiving line that funnels into the buffet line. Keep in mind that you and your parents (and whoever else is included in the receiving line) will be eating after all of your guests have gone through the line.

In many cases, the Bride and Groom (and often the Wedding Party) are served first so they can mingle and visit with their guests at their tables. But always remember to take some time to eat so you don't run out of steam yourselves.

If you will be doing a Centerpiece Give-Away Activity, the type of Meal you are serving may determine where and when it should happen. If your Meal will be a Buffet, then it should be scheduled to begin only after the Buffet line has cleared out. I once saw video footage of a band doing a popular Centerpiece Give-Away Activity that involved all of the guests at their tables, but $1/3$ of the guests were in the Buffet line and so they were completely left out. If you will be hosting a Sit-Down Meal, a good time might be right after the salad course has been served. If you will be having food stations spread throughout the room, then perhaps it would be best to do the Centerpiece Give-Away Activity just before the guests are invited to begin leaving their seats to help themselves to the food. Timing can make a big difference, while also creating some fun energy.

If you will be featuring a Video Montage/Slideshow, it can also be scheduled at several times. The first consideration will be the lighting. If your location will be flooded with daylight (an outdoor location or an indoor facility with large windows), then the timing for your slideshow will need to be measured against the time that the sun is expected to set. The Video Montage/Slideshow can be shown as a precursor to your Grand Entrance or after the Cake Cutting. But one of the best times for a Video Montage/Slideshow is just as the Meal is beginning to end. At this point, your guests are still seated and they will be ready to enjoy the presentation.

For your Special Dances, there are several options to consider as well. Taking your regional agenda expectations into account, you may want to kick off your First Dance right after your Grand Entrance or you may want to save it until the end of the Meal. When your special dances are grouped together at the end of the Meal, too many of them set back to back may start to make your guests feel restless. If your regional agenda calls for dancing between the courses of the Meal, then kicking off each new segment of open dancing with another Special Dance can spread out your Special Dances.

In my region (Southern California), it is typical to save the Special Dances until the end of the Meal. But I have seen couples successfully kick off their First Dance right after the Grand Entrance and even do the Father/Daughter and/or Mother/Son Dances while the guests are eating their salads. At a fantastic wedding reception in New Jersey, in August of 2005, the guests joined the dancing right after the Bride and Groom's Grand Entrance and First Dance. After 20 minutes of energetic dancing, everyone was seated for the Formal Toast and the salad course. Next was the Father/Daughter Dance, leading into another 20 minutes of lively dancing. Then everyone resumed their seats once again for the entrée course, during which time we did the Centerpiece Give-Away Activity. After that, we started the Mother/Son Dance which segued into the next fun-filled 20 minutes of dancing. Finally, the dancing stopped one last time for the Cake Cutting and the dessert course. A couple who was celebrating their 10th Anniversary led off the final segment of dancing with a slow song dedication that just happened to have been their First Dance song. Trying to make that happen in Southern California would be difficult, to say the least, due to regional norms.

As mentioned earlier, your Cake Cutting can occur before the Meal, after the Meal, or even a little later in the celebration. Taking your regional considerations into account, this still really comes down to your own preferences. Some will say, *"Cut the cake early so your make-up will still look good and the two of you won't be sweating in your photos."* Others will say, *"Cut the cake as the meal is ending. Serve it as dessert."* And some will even say to cut the cake as late as possible because *"Guests often wait to leave until after the Cake Cutting."* The truth is, the guests will leave after the Cake Cutting...but only if they are not being entertained, don't feel included, or are not enjoying themselves.

"The truth is, the guests will leave after the Cake Cutting ...but only if they are not being entertained, don't feel included, or are not enjoying themselves."

I often recommend scheduling the Cake Cutting to take place about 45 minutes after the meal has ended so the guests can get involved in some fun dancing before they start feeling restless. Granted, this may work in conjunction with my regional norms and might not be appropriate or advisable in other regions. However, one thing that I have noticed over the years is that when the cake is served right at the end of the Meal, it tends to go uneaten to a large degree, as most of the guests may still feel rather full. But when it is served 45 minutes after the Meal, following a good calorie burning workout on the dance floor, a larger percentage of guests will eat most, if not all, of their cake.

What about scheduling for the Money Dance/Dollar Dance? I will cover several alternative ways to present this event in much greater detail in Chapter 21: "The Money Dance/Dollar Dance." As for the timing, here are a few key points to consider. If your Money Dance/Dollar Dance will be set to slow or moderate music selections, then it is important to recognize that this event will be more of a low energy moment. Also, if you have a large guest count (200 or more), your Money Dance/Dollar Dance could stretch out and last longer than 20 minutes. You could always ask your Best Man and Maid of Honor to help regulate the lines, so your guests will be filtered through in a timely manner. If your music selections for this event will be more upbeat, then you might be able to do the Money Dance/Dollar Dance during your Open Dancing. But if the low energy example is more in line with your plans, I would recommend scheduling to do this just after your Cake Cutting. This way all of your guests will have something to do. Those that want to, can participate in your Money Dance/Dollar Dance, while those that don't, or have already participated, can take a moment to enjoy some cake. Scheduling to do a slower Money Dance/Dollar Dance during or following your Open Dancing can cause problems as the sharp dip in energy may lead your guests to perceive that the celebration is waning, which may cause them to consider leaving earlier than you might have desired.

When and where should you schedule to do your Bouquet & Garter Toss events? I will cover several alternative ways to present these events in much greater detail in Chapter 22: "The Bouquet & Garter Toss." As discussed earlier, your regional agenda expectations may need to be considered. Some may say to do the Bouquet & Garter Toss right at the end of the Meal, maybe after the Cake Cutting and just before the Special Dances. Others may say to save them until much later in your celebration. But, if the number of guests present begins to drop, you could be left with fewer participants than you might have wanted. Keeping in mind that when these events are done well, the Bouquet & Garter Toss can really create some fun energy. So, it might be wise to place them after a lower energy event, like your Cake Cutting or the Money Dance/Dollar Dance in an effort get your guests ready to resume more open dancing. Another idea would be to pass on the traditional method of requiring that only the single people can participate, and instead do the Bouquet & Garter Toss during the open dancing with no stipulations on who may or may not be eligible to catch them when they are tossed.

When it comes to scheduling your Open Dancing, we have already explored many examples of where it can be placed in your agenda. Once again, your regional norms may play a large role in determining when, where, and how much open dancing you will be able to place into your scripted timeline. If your region is primarily familiar with dancing from the very beginning between each of the meal courses, attempting to make your guests wait until the end of the Meal might be a challenging endeavor. Likewise, attempting to create fun dancing from the beginning in a region like mine, where the guests don't expect to get started until well after meal, could prove nearly impossible. Clearly discussing these issues with your reception director during your planning process will most likely prove to be very helpful. Just because your desires may not fit with your regional norms, doesn't mean that you can't or shouldn't ever attempt to try something new. The agenda displayed on the next page for Anderson & Maggie's reception was completely foreign for the regional expectations held by their guests. But with some careful planning, it not only worked, it was a huge success.

Finally, we need to consider when it will be appropriate to call it a night and do your Last Dance. If you plan to stay at your reception until the Last Dance (some couples have opted to sneak out early), keep in mind that the ending can be one of the most creative and memorable moments your guests will experience. I will cover that subject in greater detail in Chapters 25 and 26: "The Last Dance" and "The Big Sendoff." Simply put, your reception can last until the wee hours of the morning with your closest friends who really like to party. Or you can plan for an ending that involves most of your guests via the Last Dance and perhaps even by doing a Big Sendoff. Unless your location has a hard ending time with a short time frame, the timing for ending your reception is entirely up to you. If you want a large, memorable ending, don't get trapped into thinking that your reception has to last as long as you have access to the location. Be open to the idea of wrapping up early if doing so will create the best possible ending for your celebration.

Smoking Can Be Hazardous To Your Celebration

Suffice it to say, if you, or your new spouse, have to take cigarette breaks on a regular basis, the pacing and flow of your reception could be impacted. Especially if your reception events get delayed as a result. Limiting your cigarette breaks or wearing a nicotine patch might help.

Conclusion

After considering your regional agenda expectations and consulting with your reception director on your scripted timeline, the information presented here should help you to create a lineup for your events that will not only flow smoothly, but keep your guests entertained with the pacing and personal style you have been working so hard to generate. Don't be afraid to try something new, while keeping in mind that your overall goal is to make sure that everyone has a fantastic time.

ANDERSON & MAGGIE

October 28th, 2006
Silverado Canyon, California

The Dancing Never Stopped

Anderson & Maggie wanted their guests to enjoy a relaxed, laid back reception that would just naturally turn into a huge dancing party. They chose food stations instead of a formal meal. The 350 guests in attendance were encouraged to eat whenever they were hungry, dance whenever they were ready, and visit with Anderson & Maggie whenever they were nearby. They passed on most of the traditional events and even tossed their Bouquet & Garter during the dancing.

*Private Cake Cutting

Rather than stop the dancing for the formal Cake Cutting, Anderson & Maggie opted to cut their cake "under the radar" with no fanfare while their photographer and videographer captured their private dessert exchange. Then the guests were all treated to their own cup cakes!

RECEPTION AGENDA

5:00-6:15
Cocktail Hour
6:15
Grand Entrance
"Numb/Encore"
by Jay-Z & Linkin Park
6:30
First Dance
"An Angel Above Me"
by Tommy Tokioka
6:35
Toasts
6:50-9:00
Food Stations for Meal
7:10-10:00
Open Dancing
8:00
Maggie's Dedication
"Making Memories Of Us"
by Keith Urban
8:45
Bouquet Toss
"Girls Just Want To Have Fun"
by Cyndi Lauper
8:45
Garter Removal & Toss
"She's A Beauty"
by The Tubes
"Legs"
by ZZ Top
"Everybody Wants You"
by Billy Squier
9:00
Private Cake Cutting*
10:00
Last Dance
"You'll Accomp'ny Me"
By Bob Seger
10:00-10:30
After Party

CHAPTER 12

PREPARING A "PLAN B"
Putting Together a Strategy for Navigating Unexpected Circumstances

John Lennon has often been quoted for writing the following poignant line, "*Life is what happens to you while you're busy making other plans.*"[1] This proverb also holds true for creating successful reception celebrations. Even the best laid plans can get foiled when "life happens." Lucky for us, we can predict some of the common mishaps that may occur, which gives us the opportunity to prepare some "Plan B" solutions before they are needed. It is said that airline pilots are not really trained to fly planes as the planes practically fly themselves these days. Rather, they are paid well and put through rigorous training procedures so that when, and if, "life happens," they are prepared to solve whatever predictable mishaps could occur in a cool, calm, and professional manner. Applying this same methodology to your plans will not only help you to feel more prepared, but it will also help relieve any added stress caused when, and if, a predictable mishap should occur. In this chapter, we'll explore some common mishaps that are rather predictable and some wise options for creating effective "Plan B" solutions in advance.

Blame It On the Rain

One couple I had the pleasure of working with in May of 2001, shared a cute video with me which was a documentary about the planning that had gone into their wedding and reception celebration. We all got a good laugh during the scene where Jenny was researching the weather conditions for their date and region online. Even though her research said rain was only a remote possibility, we all remembered how the rain had indeed come. What could have spelled certain doom for most outdoor receptions was averted thanks to the great "Plan B" provided by their unique location. Their ceremony and reception had been set outdoors with no covering from the elements. But fortunately, their location also had a large indoor reception hall available. When a slight drizzle began falling towards the end of the meal, we quickly moved to "Plan B" and everyone moved inside within 15 minutes, just in time to start the dancing. Their celebration went a hour overtime and everyone said they were having the time of their lives.

Inclement weather can put a real damper on a reception celebration. It is vital to have a "Plan B" in place should the weather become an issue for your location. Some outdoor facilities may already have tent vendors who are on call for last minute changes due to undesirable conditions.

But undesirable weather is not just limited to rain or snow. Extremely high or low temperatures can also cause unexpected problems. If your reception hall has no air conditioning, and your summer wedding date experiences record heat levels, your guests may begin to feel like they are melting as a result. An outdoor celebration on a clear evening with unexpectedly cold conditions can cause big problems. If your location can provide portable space heaters, or even a fully enclosed tent with forced air heating, your guests will be more comfortable and they will hopefully be less likely to leave early for the warmth of their homes.

Unexpected Delays

Delays can be one of the most common obstacles for creating a successful reception celebration. But many of them can be prevented. However, it is still wise to prepare a "Plan B" for your agenda that may include moving some of your events around in order to create more energy sooner, or to ensure that the desired amount of time for open dancing will still be achievable. I have seen weddings delayed because the photographer took twice as long as expected with the post-ceremony formal photos, or because the location was unable to "turn the room" fast enough due to a previous event that may have run late, or perhaps an important family member or even a Wedding Party member was late in arriving to the ceremony or the reception. When "life happens" in instances like these, your "Plan B" solutions should give you the peace of mind to let go of any anxiety.

In August of 1999, I ran into an unexpected delay when the guests began arriving at the reception location almost a full hour after they were expected. The ceremony had taken place about 20 miles away from the reception location which was on the harbor in Dana Point. It was a beautiful Saturday afternoon and everyone in Orange County had opted to go to the beach that day. But, not just any beach. Apparently, they were all on their way to Dana Point at the same time. This caused the guests to be held up in massive traffic delays that were completely unexpected. Needless to say, I began to get worried because the wedding party was going to be about 45 minutes behind their guests, due to photos. The buffet was already set up, the food was ready, and the guests of honor were running even later than their guests. Having their location scheduled from only 12:00pm to 4:00pm, with no possibility of going overtime, I knew a solid "Plan B" was the only way we would be able to save this reception. When Kevin & Athena finally arrived, they were understandably upset since it was already 2:00pm and they now had less than 2 hours to turn their reception into a fun celebration. I had already taken the liberty of inviting their guests to begin eating much earlier. My advice for Kevin & Athena was to pass on eating so we could get through their reception events more quickly. We still had 45 minutes left for open dancing after doing a Grand Entrance, Toasts, First Dance, Father/Daughter & Mother/Son Dances, Combined Parents & Wedding Party Dances, Cake Cutting, Money Dance, and the Bouquet & Garter Toss. The pacing was certainly rushed, but it was still a fun reception.

Not Feeling Too Well?

Health issues, although thankfully rare in occurrence, can still bring a rousing celebration to a screeching halt. The worst case scenarios can include death and/or serious injury. I personally know a DJ in Southern California who has been the entertainer at three separate receptions over the course of his career where an invited guest suffered a heart attack and died as a result. Although such dire circumstances have thankfully never occurred at one of my receptions, I am fully aware that "life happens." In the highly unlikely event of an untimely death or serious injury occurring at a reception, the celebration could end early, and in the least favorable way possible. However, having personally experienced a few unexpected health issues with guests at weddings over the years, I have learned some simple, "Plan B" methods for continuing the celebration in spite of some non-tragic events that could have easily ended the party.

At a wedding reception in May of 2006, the Groom's mother suffered a serious allergic reaction to something she had eaten at the reception. An ambulance came to treat her and they helped her regain the ability to breathe more normally. But in the meantime, the Bride and Groom, and about ⅓ of their guests were outside tending to the Groom's mother. The rest of the guests inside were slowly becoming aware of what was happening, and as they had been expecting the Cake Cutting to begin soon, they were getting understandably restless. After being apprised of the situation, I moved into "Plan B" and changed the music to something mellow while letting the guests know that we were going to be delayed and asking them to be patient until this current crisis could be properly resolved. I also invited those who felt inclined to do so to offer up a prayer or two for the Groom's mother and her speedy recovery. When she was finally stabilized, the paramedics took her to the hospital just to be safe, and the Bride and Groom and their guests slowly came filtering back into the reception. The Groom was understandably distressed by what had just taken place, but he was also surrounded by his closest friends and family members who were there to support him. The celebration resumed, they cut their cake and they even danced with their guests for a short time before wrapping up with a Last Dance. Choosing to be candid with the guests not only helped keep them from leaving early, but it also empowered them to shower the Bride and Groom with positive support when they returned to their reception.

Conclusion

Discuss your concerns about the possible mishaps that might occur at your reception with your reception director during your planning process. Most of the things that can possibly go wrong at a wedding reception are somewhat predictable. Don't wait until the moment hits and get caught off guard. Make your plans as complete as possible by formulating your "Plan B" solutions so you can be confident that inclement weather, unexpected delays, and minor health concerns won't cause your plans to be ruined.

CHAPTER 13

INFORMING YOUR TEAM
Keeping Your Reception Vendors on the Same Page

Your wedding vendors should be the all-stars that will do whatever they can to make sure your reception will be a fantastic and entertaining success. But in order to effectively make that happen, they will all need to be updated with the latest information from the scripted timelines for your ceremony and/or reception. They will also need to keep communicating with each other about your upcoming events throughout your celebration. Especially if there are any last minute changes. In this chapter, we will discuss how this necessary dialogue can be accomplished in the most effective manner possible.

Phone, Fax, or E-Mail?

In today's technologically advanced world, staying in constant contact has become faster and much more convenient. You will undoubtedly be collecting contact information on your various wedding vendors so you can reach them quickly whenever the need arises. But don't stop there. Be sure to share that contact information list with your other vendors. Especially the vendors who will be the most involved in the actual production of your reception celebration. These may include your ceremony minister, your location manager, your catering manager, your wedding coordinator, your entertainment, your photographer, your videographer, and/or your reception director. Whenever possible, try to gather not only a phone number and/or a fax number, but be sure to ask for an e-mail address as well. It can also be helpful to get cell phone numbers. A physical mailing address can be helpful, but these days a web site address will often provide all of the necessary contact information for a given vendor in one convenient place.

It may also be helpful to get the name of the actual person who will be representing each vendor on your wedding day. Some photography services have a team of photographers that they send out, so if the owner won't be personally shooting your pictures, it would be very beneficial to get that person's name in advance. An all too common practice among wedding DJs involves sending a sub-contractor in the place of the actual DJ you may be expecting. Be sure to insist that the DJ who will be performing be named on your contract. Also, getting their personal contact information (i.e. cell phone number, e-mail address) would be highly recommended. In September of 2003, at a Rehearsal, I watched as a Bride was surprisingly introduced for the first time to the location coordinator who had put in charge of overseeing her Ceremony and Reception. Relying on a stranger made her understandably apprehensive.

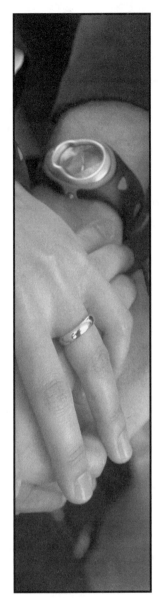

Who's Going to Make the Calls?

If you have a professional wedding coordinator assisting you with your planning, they may be the main person you want contacting the rest of your team on your behalf about the ceremony and/or reception agendas. If you don't have a wedding coordinator managing these details for you, perhaps your Master of Ceremonies will be willing to contact the rest of your team about the agendas. If you have chosen someone to serve as your reception director, that person should be eager to make these calls so they can make sure the rest of your team are fully up to speed. If you have secured a Wedding Entertainment Director™, he or she will certainly request a copy of your vendors contact information list so they can share your final ceremony and/or reception agendas with the rest of your team. They will be ready to answer any questions your vendors may have about your agendas. They will also ask them if they would like to make any additions or changes to your agendas, such as adding in a group photo. However, if you will be managing your planning details on your own, it is still vitally important for your entire team of vendors to receive advance contact from you regarding your scripted timelines.

Keeping Everyone in the Loop

During your reception celebration, it will be very important for your team of vendors to be kept informed about which event will be coming up next and any possible changes that may be taking place as well. On your wedding day, you will not be able to manage the important duties of keeping your team working together effectively. That's one reason why it is very important to select vendors who are "team players," meaning they're accustomed to keeping each other updated. If you have a wedding coordinator, they may be ready to manage the rest of your team. If you have a Master of Ceremonies, they may also be prepared to keep your other vendors in the loop before starting any new events. If you have a Wedding Entertainment Director™, they will certainly take the time to communicate throughout your celebration with your vendors.

It can also be helpful to lay down some simple ground rules that can prevent miscommunications or missed opportunities. One simple ground rule is that your team leader (whoever you have selected to serve as your reception director) should be directly notified by your other vendors before they leave the room for any reason. If the Bride and Groom are ready for their First Dance, but the Videographer cannot be located in a timely manner, the First Dance may get delayed as a result. If the Photographer wants to take the Bride and Groom outside for sunset photos, but your team leader is not notified or given an ETA on their return, the team leader may be left wondering where they are. Such a situation can lead to further delays in the reception agenda as the team leader may have to go on a search for the missing guests of honor. I once had a location coordinator who got upset with me for starting the Cake Cutting without her. The Bride had insisted on starting the Cake Cutting a little sooner than either of us had anticipated. And so, after making several fruitless attempts to find the location coordinator to let her know, I informed the rest of the team and then I made several announcements that we were about to do the Cake Cutting. I was hoping that she would hear my announcements, wherever she was, and be ready to assist them as needed. As my luck would have it, she came running in from the kitchen just after the Bride and Groom had begun to cut their cake. If she would have followed this simple ground rule for effective team communication, perhaps I would have known where to find her and an uncomfortable misunderstanding could have been prevented.

Getting Lost in the Crowd

If your guest count is rather large, it may become difficult for your team leader (reception director) to locate the rest of your vendors, when needed, amongst your guests. Another simple ground rule for keeping your team on the same page would be to encourage all of the team members to make regular eye contact with each other and especially with your Master of Ceremonies. In a large crowd, sometimes just being able to make eye contact and exchange some simple hand signals from across the room can be all that is needed to ensure that the whole team is ready to begin the next important event.

Andy Austin, a popular wedding entertainer in the Dallas/Forth Worth area, came up with an ingeniously simple way to keep his fellow wedding vendors, and even his VIPs, informed in overly large crowds. He uses mini text pagers controlled by his own computer system so he can send out a text message that might say, "Best Man's Toast in 10 minutes!" Your entire team of vendors (and even the Best Man) will be instantly notified silently on their own vibrating, mini pagers, which were provided to them before the reception began.

Conclusion

Keeping your team on the same page will go a long way towards creating a fun reception that will flow smoothly, while preventing conflicts or miscommunication from occurring between your vendors. Make sure to choose the person who will serve as your team leader wisely. Look for someone who knows how to think about your entire team's needs, instead of just their own. If your Master of Ceremonies has demonstrated the skills and the ability to serve effectively as the team leader (reception director), they would be the best choice for that role. If they are not prepared for those responsibilities, your wedding coordinator or the location's catering manager may be your best fit. However, if you have secured a Wedding Entertainment Director™, he or she will certainly be prepared, experienced, and willing to serve as the team leader (reception director) while remaining a true team player.

"Look for someone on your team who knows how to think about your entire team's needs, instead of just their own."

PART III

ADDING YOUR PERSONAL STYLE
Putting Your Fingerprints on Every Page of Your Reception Plan

The most unique part of any reception is the bride and the groom.
Almost all receptions have a cake and flowers and decorations
and tuxedos and dresses and food and linens and photographs.
But your guests won't be attending to see any of those things.
Your guests will be there to see you, to congratulate you,
to celebrate with you, and to laugh and cry with you.
This section will feature the memorable moments that
your guests will be talking about for years to come.

The ideas in this section will range from the simple to the highly complex and will be scored as follows:

★	★★	★★★	★★★★	★★★★★
Total Novice	Some Skill Needed	Skilled & Talented	Very Talented	Top Level Talent
These are ideas that you can implement without any assistance.	These are ideas that you could pull off with practice and some training.	These are ideas that will require help from someone with basic talent.	These are ideas that will require help from someone with proven talent.	These are ideas that will require finding the very best quality talent.

CHAPTER 14

THE WEDDING CEREMONY

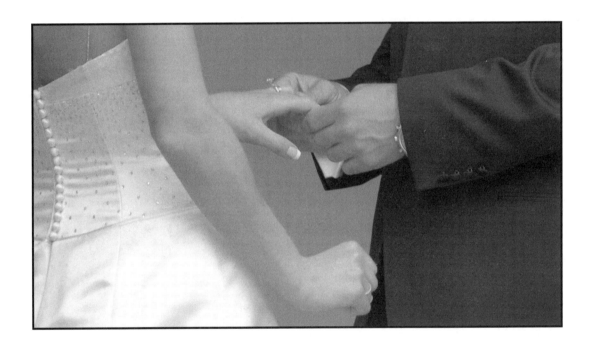

Your Wedding Ceremony will be attended by your closest friends and family. They have all been looking forward to watching as the two of you become Husband and Wife ever since they first heard the news of your engagement. The Reception that follows will merely be a celebration of the lifelong commitment you will be making. Your choices for your Ceremony can and will be the precursor that lets your guests know what kind of reception celebration they are about to experience. Whether your choices will lean towards traditional or non-traditional ideas, you should feel free to put your personal touches into each and every aspect of your Wedding Ceremony.

Here Comes The Bride ★

One of the first questions that will come to mind relates to your musical selections. Will you be choosing traditional, classical selections for your Processionals and Recessional? Will you be choosing non-traditional music for those moments? Or will you be using a little of both? If your theme will be traditional, keep in mind that there are many different versions of the traditional, classical pieces, such as the ever popular "Canon in D Major" by Johann Pachelbel. That piece sounds quite different on a harp, on a piano, or even when it is performed by an orchestra. If non-traditional selections will be more your style, feel free to get creative and do what will fit best for you.

In a July of 2006 ceremony, the Bride and Groom picked out their own non-traditional musical selections. The Mothers were escorted forward and seated to "Maybe I'm Amazed" by Jem. The Minister, the Groom, and his Groomsmen all came strolling in while "Little Green Bag" by The George Baker Selection was playing. This song had been selected as it is the opening theme from one of the Groom's favorite movies, "Reservoir Dogs." Then the Bridesmaids came forward while a specially edited loop of "Bittersweet Symphony" by The Verve was playing. Finally, the Bride was escorted down the aisle by her Father to the ballad, "Angel Standing By" by Jewel. When the Ceremony ended and the Minister introduced them as Husband and Wife, they exited down the aisle to "Ring Of Fire" by Social Distortion.

Bonus Chapters! As an added special bonus for purchasing this book, you can download 4 free Bonus Chapters. One of them is a detailed list of Ceremony Music Suggestions. Simply register at:
TheBestWeddingReceptionEver.com

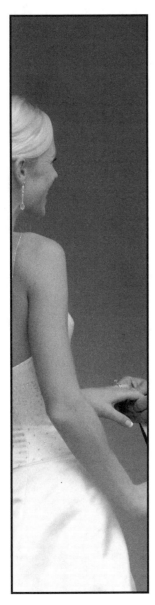

Write Your Own Vows ★

In addition to, or in place of, the vows your minister will be using during the Ceremony, you could write and recite your own vows to each other. It could be something as simple as a list of the things you truly love about each other. Or it could be heartfelt promises that have been written in your own voice, incorporating your unique style, your personality, your emotions, and maybe even your sense of humor. But, make sure your voices will be properly amplified so your guests will be able to enjoy this moment with you.

Have Someone Give a Special Reading ★

This can be a great way to involve someone special who was not included in your Wedding Party. There are a variety of resources to choose from. Whether you select a passage of scripture from the Bible, a poem, or even a few lines of Shakespeare, this option can add a more personalized feeling to your Ceremony. Also, be sure to ask for an additional microphone so your guests will all be able to hear your reader.

Have Someone Sing a Special Song ★★★

If you have a close friend or family member who loves to sing, and can sing well, this can be great way to let them play an important role in your Ceremony. Make sure they have their own music (an accompaniment track) and be sure to also request an additional microphone so your guests will all be able to hear. They might also want a chance to rehearse before the guests begin to arrive. Rehearsal arrangements should be discussed with your entertainment vendors in advance.

The Binding/"Hand Fasting" Ceremony ★★★

This creative idea involves your minister using a small rope to "bind" your hands together while making a series of promises to one another. After each promise of love is made, more rope is entwined around your hands until you have both been symbolically secured to one another.

Light a Unity Candle ★★

This idea can create a symbolic act that will represent your new union as Husband and Wife. You can even ask your Mothers to get involved by having them light the two outer candles you will use later to light the Unity Candle. If your Ceremony will take place outdoors, be sure to check out the wind conditions, and consider providing hurricane covers so the candles will stay lit. If it is not already provided, you will need to bring a lighter of some kind. Having small votive candles already lit on the table can create a much nicer look than using lighters to ignite the outer candles. Also, this might be good moment for a special song to play in the background.

The Sand Ceremony ★★

This idea can also create a symbolic act that will represent your new union as husband and wife, much like the Unity Candle, and may be perfect for outdoor settings that are too windy for lit candles. Taking two different vessels (vases, sea shells, antique bottles, etc.) that have been filled with two different colors of sand, the Bride and Groom will be instructed to pour their separate containers of sand into one larger container (preferably one that is made of clear glass) creating a mixed pattern. Additional vessels with additional containers can be added for children and/or step children so they can be invited to participate as well. Also, this might be a good moment for a special song in the background.

Present Promises to Step-Children ★★

If either of you have children from a previous relationship, then you will be creating a blended family. Taking a moment to express a separate commitment to your new step-children in the form of personalized promises and/or presenting them with a commemorative item (such as a medallion, bracelet, etc.) can make your Ceremony more personally unique. It will also make your future step-children feel included in a very special way. Also, this might be good moment for a special song to play in the background. If you would like your guests to enjoy this moment with you, make sure your voices will be properly amplified. Or, you can arrange to have the microphones muted if you would prefer to keep this special moment private.

Blessing the Rings ★★★★

With a long piece of satin ribbon that's quickly strewn down each row of guests, starting from one side of the aisle and coming back down the other, your rings can be passed down the thread so that each person can touch them briefly in a symbolic act of blessing your rings. This idea is a little complicated, but it will allow every guest to be an active participant in your Ceremony. Also, this might be good moment for a special song to play in the background.

The Surprise Ring Bearer ★★★

When your Minister asks for the Rings, the Best Man will act caught off guard and begin patting down his pockets. Suddenly, a fanfare of music begins to play as a special friend who had not been included, comes down the aisle, presenting the rings on a pillow for all to see.

Present Roses to Your Mothers ★

Take a moment during your Ceremony to present your Mothers with a long stem rose in a symbolic gesture of your gratitude. Also, this might be a good moment for a special song to play in the background.

Honor the Dearly Departed ★

Take a moment during your Ceremony to honor any dearly departed loved ones, especially recently deceased parents and/or grandparents. This can be done with the lighting of commemorative candles, reserving an empty chair on the front row for them, and optionally placing a rose or a bouquet on it. Also, this might be a good moment for a special song to play in the background.

Flower Petal Toss ★

Provide paper cones filled with flower petals on the inside ends of each row of chairs or pews. Then have your Minister instruct your guests to get them ready just before he introduces you as Husband and Wife and sends you down the aisle. While you are making your exit, they can shower you with flower petals.

Butterfly Release ★★

Provide each guest with a small paper box holding a monarch butterfly. Then have your Minister instruct your guests to get them ready just before he introduces you as Husband and Wife and sends you down the aisle. While you are making your exit, the butterflies will be released. Securing the butterflies and keeping them alive can be a little precarious, but the moment created when they are released can be quite striking.

Dove Release ★★★

The Bride and Groom are presented with live Doves to hold in their hands while the Minister shares how their release symbolizes your new beginning as Husband and Wife. Then the Doves are released as your guests cheer.

Bring in a Live Bagpiper ★★★★

Nothing fills the air with a feeling of electricity quite like the sound of Bagpipes. A live Bagpiper can make your Ceremony Processional and/or Recessional into a truly memorable moment. You won't need to worry about amplification, as bagpipes are naturally loud enough on their own.

MARK & MELISSA

August 5th, 2005
Ringwood, New Jersey

"Mazel Tov!"

With a last name like Pedalino, it's fairly obvious that Mark is Italian. However, as a popular Bar/Bat Mitzvah Entertainer, his respect for the Jewish traditions were evident during their Wedding Ceremony. Mark was escorted forward by his Father and Mother. Melissa was also escorted down the aisle by her Mom and Dad. Finally, before they were presented as Husband and Wife, Mark stepped down firmly on the glass to break it as their guests all shouted..."Mazel Tov!"

*"Crazy Little Thing Called Love"

Being a highly skilled DJ Entertainer himself, Mark selected "Crazy Little Thing Called Love" by Michael Bublé to play as his Groomsmen entered, followed by Queen's version of the same song mixed in at the A Capella break as Mark made his own entrance...and then the guests all cheered!

CEREMONY AGENDA

5:00-6:30
Drinks & Appetizers

6:30
Guests Begin Seating
"Bolero"
by Maurice Ravel

6:40
Ceremony Begins

Seating of Grandparents
"Canon In D Major"
by Johann Pachelbel

Groomsmen's Processional
"Crazy Little Thing Called Love"
by Michael Bublé

Groom's Processional
"Crazy Little Thing Called Love"
by Queen

Bridesmaid's Processional
"These Are Days"
by 10,000 Maniacs

Bride's Processional
"You Are So Beautiful"
by Joe Cocker

Ceremony
Officiated by:
Rev. Randy Bartlett

Nuptial Blessing
Read by:
Grandma Dora Pedalino

7:20
Recessional
"Then He Kissed Me"
by The Crystals
"Finally"
by Ce Ce Peniston

7:30
Off to the Reception!

CHAPTER 15

THE COCKTAIL HOUR

While you are finishing formal photos after the Ceremony, the guests will be patiently waiting for your arrival at the Reception. This period of time is usually called the Cocktail Hour because the bar is now open and, often, refreshments are being served. But will an open bar and a few hors d'oeuvres be enough to keep your guests entertained during that time? The answer is commonly "yes," but this chapter will explore some creative ideas that can make the Cocktail Hour even more memorable.

Background Music Sets the Mood ★★

Drinks and appetizers will give your guests something to drink and eat. But the Cocktail Hour may feel dry and uninviting without some music. When appropriate background music is playing, the atmosphere it creates will make your guests feel more comfortable. Perhaps you will have a string quartet or jazz group that will play for your Ceremony and your Cocktail Hour. If you have chosen to hire a DJ, or you have secured a Wedding Entertainment Director™, then choosing appropriate music selections to play during your Cocktail Hour will be important. Keep in mind that your selections should create the kind of ambiance that will match your personal style, while complimenting any themes you may have chosen for your Wedding Reception. Music that is too loud or would be described as obnoxious by most of your guests should be avoided in favor of music that is unobtrusive and pleasing to the ear.

One couple in June of 2005 had decided on a 40's theme for the Bride's hair and gown, the Bridesmaids' hair and dresses, and even the décor. Putting together a mix of classic Vocal Jazz artists like Frank Sinatra, Dean Martin, Ella Fitzgerald, Nat King Cole, and Billie Holiday, while featuring their best songs about love, was a perfect match.

In April of 2006, one couple requested a fun mix of Alternative listening hits from the 1980's to entertain their guests during their Cocktail Hour. Songs like "Bette Davis Eyes" by Kim Carnes, "Down Under" by Men At Work, "Steppin' Out" by Joe Jackson, and "99 Red Balloons" by Nena filled the air. The guests started getting the idea that they would be in for a fun celebration in just a little while.

Bonus Chapters! As an added special bonus for purchasing this book, you can download 4 free Bonus Chapters. One of them is a detailed list of Background Music Suggestions. Simply register at:
TheBestWeddingReceptionEver.com

Everybody Loves a Chocolate Fountain ★★

When the smell of melted chocolate begins to fill the air, your guests' mouths will begin to water. With sliced fruit, marshmallows, graham crackers, and rice crispy treats for dipping, your friends and family members will enjoy a light dessert while they await your arrival.

Disposable Cameras ★

Let your guests pass around some disposable cameras so they can take fun photos of their own. When the reception is over, you get to collect all of the cameras and then see what develops. Ask the MC to remind the guests to leave the spent cameras on their tables. The MC can also offer the guests some basic instructions, including how to activate the flash. On a side note, be sure to get quality, name brand disposable cameras, as some of the cheaper, generic brands tend to turn out considerably fewer quality images per camera.

Autographs on Your Engagement Portrait ★

Provide a framed engagement portrait on an easel with a matte border and then invite your guests to leave their autographs on it for a keepsake. This idea can be carried over to other items as well. One couple provided the guests with a special marker so they could autograph a surfboard. When my wife, Lisa, and I got married in December of 1994, we had a friend make up a large, white, vinyl banner with our names and wedding date printed on it. Our guests enjoyed signing their names all over it.

The Polaroid/Scrapbook Guest Book ★★

Enlist the services of a friend or family member to take Polaroid pictures of each person, couple, or family in attendance, and then invite them to write a special message for the Bride and Groom on the page adjacent to their instant photo. This can also be done using a digital camera with a compatible printer. This idea can be used with stickers and markers to make a scrapbook that has been created by all of your guests.

Bring in a Photo Booth ★★★

Rent a Photo Booth for the day and invite your guests to sit inside and get their pictures taken. Whether they decide to make goofy faces or just pose with friendly smiles, they can then cut and paste their fun pictures into a scrapbook and write a personalized note to the Bride and Groom.

I personally saw a Photo Booth keep the guests entertained for the entire evening at a reception in November of 2006. Even the Bride and Groom stepped inside to take some photos while feeding each other cake. More information on renting a Photo Booth for your Reception can be found at this web site: (PhotoBoothScrapbooks.com)

Words of Wisdom Cards ★

Provide note cards, pens, and a receptacle with instructions for your guests to fill out the cards. Have them put their names on one side and their best words of wisdom on how to have a long and happy marriage on the other. When they are done, the cards can be placed in a small box or treasure chest as a keepsake. They can also be used to fill a scrapbook.

Bride & Groom Trivia Mixer ★

Write up a list of 10 to 20 unique things about the two of you that are only known by one person each amongst your group of guests. Print up the list of questions with blanks for the answers that can be filled in by your guests. Be sure to clarify on the listed instructions that the answers are only known by one person per question. This will certainly keep the participants busy as they will have to ask most, if not all, of your guests for the answers they are seeking. You might even offer a prize to the first person who can get all of the correct answers. Print off enough copies for everyone and have them set out at the Cocktail Hour. Those that participate will not only learn more about the two of you in the process, but they will also get to know quite a few of your guests.

Display a Looped Video Montage ★★

Have your videographer, your DJ, or a friend create a short video montage about the two of you and set it to repeat continuously, on a small television, monitor, or a laptop screen, throughout your Cocktail Hour. If you already have background music playing, then muting the audio portion of the video montage would be recommended.

Bring in a Magician ★★★★

When one of your guests suddenly makes a coin disappear using slight of hand, the guests who are nearby will realize they may be in for a treat. Magicians who specialize in close up magic tricks can blend into your crowd putting on spontaneous, mini performances for groups of 5 to 10 at a time. Soon your crowd will be buzzing with conversation with the most commonly overheard question being, "How did he do that?"

Creative Photos for Table Numbers ★★

Jim Cerone, a popular wedding entertainer in Indianapolis, IN, says, *"Create your own table numbers featuring photos of the two of you in a variety of fun and meaningful locations. Have a friend snap the photos during an afternoon road trip from one site to the next while you hold up a hand painted sign with a different table number at each location. When your guests see these, they will soon begin making new friends as they wander the room to see the different photos that have been created for each table."*[1]

CHAPTER 16

THE GRAND ENTRANCE

Many entertainers believe that loud music and even louder introductions are the key ingredients for creating a memorable performance. Although such a performance may be memorable, it might not be memorable for the right reasons. Your Grand Entrance will set the tone for the rest of your reception celebration. If this moment is used to create connections that are informative, entertaining, personalized, and emotional; your guests will feel more involved and they will have more fun. In this chapter, we will examine how you can make your introductions unique, humorous, creative, and even dramatic. Let's make it Grand!

Just the Two of Us ★★

The simplest Grand Entrance involves just introducing the two of you into the Reception while your guests are encouraged to stand and cheer. This is a moment your guests have been waiting for and they will greet you both with smiles and applause.

Meet the Parents ★★★

Taking a moment to properly introduce your Parents provides an opportunity for showing them some much deserved gratitude. If either of your Parents are divorced and/or remarried, be sure to clarify with your MC how and in what order you would like them to be introduced. These introductions can be simply asking them to stand at their tables as the guests applaud, or they can be invited to enter the room as they are announced, preceding the Wedding Party's introductions.

The Little Angels ★★★

If you will have a Flower Girl(s) and/or a Ring Bearer(s), and they are ready for this kind of moment in the spotlight, feel free to have them introduced as well. You might also need someone in the room who is ready to collect them so they don't get overwhelmed and become unsure about where to go.

It's Raining Men! ★★★

If you will have Ushers seating guests at your Ceremony that will not be in your Wedding Party of Bridesmaids and Groomsmen, feel free to have them introduced before bringing in your wedding party.

Here Comes the Wedding Party ★★★

It can be lots of fun to introduce your wedding party of bridesmaids and groomsmen into the reception. You can have them introduced as couples working through the lineup and ending with your Best Man and Maid of Honor. They can be introduced one person at a time, alternating the bridesmaids with the groomsmen. You could have them come in all at once as one big group. Or, you could introduce the bridesmaids one at a time, followed by the groomsmen one at a time.

Create Some Energy With Theme Music ★★★

Rather than just making these introductions as announcements, make this a production by adding theme music. You can choose a dramatic theme song that will start playing just as the two of you enter the room. You can select a separate theme song to play as your Wedding Party is being introduced. You can even pick out theme songs for your Parents, the Ushers, and the Ring Bearer and Flower Girl. This can be personalized even further by choosing a different song for each couple in your Wedding Party. You can even pick out a theme song for each individual in your Wedding Party, maybe even a song that really sums up their personality or what they do for a living. You may need to discuss your theme song ideas with your entertainment vendor to make sure they own, or can play, the songs you are requesting. Also, you may want to clearly communicate where you want the songs to begin. I once watched a DJ on video introduce the Bride's Parents to "Jesse's Girl" by Rick Springfield, as her Father was named Jesse. But the song starts off soft and it was faded out well before it got to the title portion of the chorus. Most of the guests missed the homage to the Bride's Father's name because the DJ started the song from the beginning rather than selecting a cue point that would have been more meaningful and more energetic.

> ***Bonus Chapters!*** As an added special bonus for purchasing this book, you can download 4 free Bonus Chapters. One of them is a detailed list of Reception Music Suggestions, including some great song ideas for Grand Entrance theme music. Simply register at:
> **TheBestWeddingReceptionEver.com**

Turn on the Spotlight ★★★★★

Lighting effects dramatically enhance a well-produced Grand Entrance. When the house lights go down and several spotlights begin spinning around the room in tempo to the music, your guests will begin to cheer before you even get in the room. Spotlights can be used to highlight the doorway where your Wedding Party will be entering. The spotlights can then follow you as you enter the room with your guests applauding. It is very important to make sure that your entertainment vendor has the right technology and expertise to produce these lighting effects properly.

The Best
Wedding
Reception
...Ever!

Attack of the Paparazzi! ★★★

This creative idea has been suggested by Scott Faver, a nationally known wedding entertainer from Phoenix, AZ. *"Have your MC instruct the guests to grab their cameras and/or any disposable cameras that have been provided and get ready to give the two of you a special welcome upon your introduction. As soon as you walk through the doors, you will be mobbed as dozens of your guests armed with cameras suddenly begin swarming around you snapping pictures as if you are rock stars and they are the paparazzi!"*[1]

Incorporate a Stylistic Theme ★★★★

How about creating a Grand Entrance that resembles other well produced introductions? Sporting Events, Movies, or Game Shows can all be sources of inspiration. Using a Basketball Theme, your Bridesmaids and Groomsmen could be introduced reciting their height and Alma Maters.

"Standing a full 6 foot 1 and hailing from Bergen Community College... show some love for our Best Man...Dave Miller!"

You could even request theme music using their College fight songs. Using a Movie Theme, your Bridesmaids and Groomsman could be introduced into the room wearing outfits from the 60's while playing songs from the Austin Powers soundtrack or from the Grease soundtrack. Using a Game Show Theme, your Bridesmaids and Groomsmen could be introduced as contestants on the Dating Game.

"An accountant by day and a party girl by night. She's a Cancer who enjoys watching re-runs of Will & Grace and taking long, moonlit walks on the beach with strange men. Let's hear it for the Maid of Honor... Lisa Forrette!"

Of course, the Dating Game theme music would be playing. You could play the theme music from Masterpiece Theater just before the two of you make your entrance, and have your MC give your guests a look back into the historical moments that occurred on your wedding date.

"On this day in history, in 1796, America welcomed it's very first Elephant. In 1899, the inventor of Scrabble was born. His name was Alfred Butts. And in 1967, The Turtles were at number 1 on the charts... with "Happy Together." But these moments all pale in comparison to the one you have all witnessed today! And now, Here they are for the very first time in recorded history...the new Mr. and Mrs. Jeremy Brown!"

Your MC will absolutely need to know how to write humor, while also demonstrating that they are highly skilled in the art of being funny without coming off as cheesy, canned, or inappropriate.

The
Grand
Entrance

1: Some of the ideas presented in this chapter may not fit for you.

2: Don't be afraid to come up with your own creative ideas.

3: It is vital that you discuss with your MC how you want these events to be presented, including reviewing scripted introductions.

4: Make sure you clearly spell out what you consider appropriate and inappropriate.

5: Each MCs level of skill and talent for presenting these introductions can vary greatly.

6: Ask for video footage to see how your MC actually presents them.

7: Be sure to discuss with your MC how and when you would like to do these introductions.

8: Make sure your MC knows how to properly pronounce any names that may be challenging.

Show Off Some Hidden Talents ★★★★★

If one or more of your Wedding Party members has a unique ability or specialized skill that could be entertaining, find a way for your MC to coax them into showcasing their hidden talents during the introductions. At a reception in March of 2005, a groomsman named Micah was well known for his own unique dance referred to as "The Micah Man Dance." I found out that he would only do this dance to an '80's rap song called "Take It To Da House" by Trick Daddy. At the right moment, the guests were told about his special dance and the music was started. Everyone began cheer and sure enough, he did "The Micah Man Dance!" Perhaps one of your Wedding Party members likes to sing karaoke to one particular song, or is a wealth of sports trivia going back decades, or can quote obscure lines from popular movies. Any of these ideas and more can be turned into a quick entertaining moment, when your Wedding Party members is given a chance to showcase their hidden talents.

Start Your Own Dance Contest ★★★

Andy Austin, a popular wedding entertainer from Dallas/Forth Worth, TX, says, *"Challenge your Wedding Party members to try and top each other with some funny dance moves as they enter the room and step onto the dance floor. If the Ushers will be entering first, get them to set the bar high by tearing off their jackets and swinging them over their heads. Each couple that follows will have to come up with their own routines and your guests will be roaring with laughter and applause."* [2] It is very important to make sure your entertainment vendor fully understands how to do this properly so it won't be presented poorly.

Personalized Biographical Introductions ★★★★★

Write a short biographical introduction for your MC to deliver about each Wedding Party member as they enter. You can include information about your relationship (relative/friend/how long), where they live, their occupation and/or educational status (i.e. college student, high school student), their relationship status (single/engaged/married), their hobbies, reasons why they might be "famous," what their friends would vote them most likely to do in life, an embarrassing story, or what their friendship means to you on a personal level. The size of your Wedding Party should determine how much detail should go into each scripted bio. If you have a large Wedding Party, keep it short so your Grand Entrance won't feel too long. It is absolutely vital that your entertainment vendor fully understands how to do this properly so it won't be presented poorly.

Introduce Your Own Wedding Party Members ★★★★

If you decide to create personalized bios, another option would be for the two of you to deliver the scripted introductions for your Wedding Party members yourselves. You will need a cordless microphone so you can read the script from outside the room. At a reception in May of 2002, the Bride and Groom chose this option. The guests were pleasantly surprised to be hearing their voices as they introduced their Wedding Party with personalized bios. Another couple in September of 2000 took this idea to a whole new level. The Groom worked in video production, so they created their own pre-recorded, personalized, biographical introductions on a DVD featuring photo-montages of them with each Wedding Party member. The Wedding Party members were able to watch their individual videos along with the guests. It is very important that you make sure your entertainment vendor fully understands how to help you do this properly so it won't be presented poorly.

Incorporate Humorous Sound Clips ★★★★★

Another layer of production quality that can be added to greatly enhance personalized biographical introductions is the use of fun sound clips. These audio clips can include: movie clips, sound effects, song clips, and special recordings. Movie clips can be used to gently poke fun at your Wedding Party. When introducing the Bride's only Brother, you could say that his first reaction to the news of their engagement sounded like this…(and then play a clip from Tommy Boy where Chris Farley says..)

"Brother?...I'm gonna have a Brother? I've always dreamed about having a Brother!"

Sound effects can be used as a punch line for a joke about how small the town is where one of the Groomsmen lives. When the sound effects of crickets chirping and cows mooing plays, the guests will enjoy a good laugh. Song clips can be used to highlight a Groomsman's occupation. If he is a stock broker, the theme song from The Apprentice, with the lyrics, "Money, Money, Money" will get a good reaction. And finally, special recordings can really create some memorable moments. At a reception in June of 2006, one of the Bridesmaids was an "On Air" reporter for her local television station. Thanks to the internet, we were able to record a short clip from one of her stories with the Anchor thanking her by name as she finished. She was completely surprised to hear her own voice and her reaction resulted in a great swell of laughter from the crowd. It is absolutely vital that you make sure your entertainment vendor fully understands how to do this properly so it won't be presented poorly. The timing issues are critical for pulling this off in a manner that will let your guests know that they are about to experience "The Best Wedding Reception…Ever!"

The
Grand
Entrance

131

CHAPTER 17

THE TOASTS

Public speaking has often been cited as one of our most common fears. The Formal Toasts at your reception will serve as an opportunity for those that are closest to you to share some sentimental anecdotes, words of appreciation, and best wishes for your secure and happy future. Some, who have been asked to make a Formal Toast, will spend countless hours writing, re-writing, and rehearsing their presentation to make sure it properly conveys their truest thoughts and feelings. Some may choose to wait until the moment they're introduced and then speak from the heart. Sadly, the latter example can often result in toasts that may feature some unexpected, and even off color comments. When it comes to preparing for a toast, Tom Haibeck, the author of "Wedding Toasts Made Easy" and "The Wedding MC," says, *"Far too many people just assume they can stand up before several hundred people and "wing it" with a wedding toast. And that's THE most common reason why wedding toasts go awry — the people delivering them simply aren't prepared. As a result, they often get nervous and flustered, become incoherent, drone on way too long, venture into areas that are completely inappropriate and embarrass themselves and others in the process."*[1] In this chapter, we will explore some creative ideas for making the Formal Toasts at your reception more polished, more memorable, and more uniquely personalized.

Pick Toasters Who Are Ready, Willing, and Able ★★

Your list should start with those who may already be expecting to make a toast, such as: the Best Man, the Maid/Matron of Honor, the Bride's Parents, the Groom's Parents, or even both of you...the Bride & Groom. Next, determine who really wants to give a toast, and who you really want (or don't want) to give a toast. Whomever you select to give a Formal Toast should be given plenty of advance notice so they can get prepared. Consider buying them a book on preparing wedding toasts as a thoughtful gift. Finally, don't be afraid to give them some guidelines regarding your thoughts on: inappropriate content, time constraints, etc.

Invite Someone Special to Give a Blessing for the Meal ★

Perhaps you'd like to include a relative or close friend in your festivities by asking them to say a Blessing for the Meal. If your Wedding Minister is a friend of the family, they might be a good choice as well.

Create the Toasting Order Based on Content ★★★★★

Randy Bartlett, a nationally known wedding entertainer based out of Sacramento, CA, says, *"The Formal Toasts will usually vary in content and delivery. By discussing what will be said in advance with each person toasting, not only can I assist them in possibly delivering their toasts better, but I can also arrange the toasting order to build towards a big punch line that will get everyone laughing, or we might start with a good laugh while leading to an emotionally poignant toast. The temperament of the Bride and Groom along with their guests will really dictate for me which toasting order will be most effective at each reception."* [2] Someone else will need to create this lineup order for you as you really shouldn't be privy to the contents of the formal toasts before they are delivered. The most obvious person to entrust this with would be your MC. But it is absolutely vital that you make sure the MC fully understands how to do this properly and most effectively.

Multi-Media Toasts ★★★★★

If one or more of your toasters would like to use an audio sound clip, such as a special recorded message, a song clip, or a movie clip, you should put them in touch with your entertainment vendor to discuss their needs and the timing for playing the clip or clips in conjunction with their toasts. The same advice holds true if they want to show a short video segment as a part of their toast. I once had a Best Man who brought in a projector with a screen at the last minute as he wanted to surprise the Bride and Groom with a video segment during his toast. This was also a big surprise to me. And as the MC, I had to help him set up and test the equipment and run the audio through my sound system. What could have been a frantic set up in the middle of toasts while the guests were becoming restless, turned out instead to be a smooth-flowing transition as I had been able to set up and test everything ahead of time during the cocktail hour.

The Key Trick ★★★★

A fun practical joke that has been done at receptions over the years is to pass out a key to several of the ladies throughout the room, and then during the toasts, someone suggests that if anyone in attendance has an old house key for the Groom's place, they should turn them in right away as he is now officially "off the market." If the Groom is kept completely unaware that this is about to occur, he will begin turning several shades of red as more and more of the female guests start streaming up one at time and dropping their keys on the head table. A good theme song could be "Just A Gigolo/I Ain't Got Nobody" by David Lee Roth. You could even give a key or two to a few men for even more laughs. This idea is best when presented by your Best Man or your Maid/Matron of Honor. Be sure your MC knows this will be happening as well and is ready with any special music cues.

Give a Welcoming Message of Thanks ★★★

Take a moment when you first enter your reception, just after the formal toasts, or right after your cake cutting, to give a welcoming message thanking your guests for being an important part of your celebration and encouraging them to have a fun time. Be sure your MC knows you will be doing this and when you'd like to do it so they can make sure you have a microphone.

Pre-Recorded Toasts ★★★

At a reception in October of 2001, the Groom's best friend (and also his first choice for Best Man) was unable to attend from the East Coast due to the events of 9/11. The Bride was able to secure a pre-recorded toast from this valued friend. When it was played during the reception, it brought tears to the Groom's eyes. If you have loved ones who won't be able to attend your reception, this can be a powerful way to include them in your celebration. Be sure your MC knows you will be doing this and when you'd like to do it as well.

"Surprise" Toasts ★★★★

Do you have one or more friends who are gifted speakers and/or are naturally funny, but they have not been included in your celebration yet? Perhaps you would enjoy putting them on the spot? The "Surprise" Toasts can really create some fun energy during the Meal. The MC will have been given the names and seating locations for your victim(s). After the Formal Toasts have finished, the guests will be informed that there are still a few more toasts coming during the Meal, but who will be giving them has not yet been determined. Then, when the guests least expect it, the MC will gather their attention while introducing the first "surprise" toaster who, although completely unprepared, will be handed a cordless microphone as the MC walks away. If you choose your victim(s) wisely, this can create some very humorous memories.

Open Invite for Guests to Toast ★★★

If you have the time and want to give your guests a chance to get in on the toasts, have your MC offer an opportunity for anyone else who might be interested to come up to the microphone and make a toast. The MC will need to be told in advance that this will be done and how long you would prefer for the open toasting to last. This idea is not advisable for toasts that are preceding a finely timed meal service as it could easily run longer than expected.

The
Toasts

CHAPTER 18

THE MEAL

One of the most overlooked moments for allowing your guests to feel more involved in your reception celebration is during the Meal. Often the entertainment vendors will take a break and throw on the same old background music they play at every wedding because, after all, people are eating so the fun can't begin until their food is gone, right? WRONG! Depending on how many courses are served and your total guest count, the Meal could last anywhere from just 45 minutes to well over 2 hours! That's a long time for your guests to be left wondering when the fun and dancing will finally get started. Don't forget, a reception is supposed to be a celebration, not just a fancy dinner. In this chapter, we will uncover several methods for adding life to the Meal while also encouraging your guests to become active participants, so they won't feel like spectators.

Background Music Can Build Energy ★★

As mentioned above, at many wedding receptions, the background music played during the meal might be best described as the "default setting." Not only is your background music not given much thought, the Bride & Groom are only provided with the typical "default setting" of music that their entertainment always plays for background during the Meal. Whether you have chosen to go with a Band, hire a DJ, or perhaps you have secured a Wedding Entertainment Director™, the Background Music choices that will play during the Meal should be yours and yours alone. Keep in mind that your selections should start to build some energy in a manner that will match your personal style, while complimenting any themes you may have chosen for your Wedding Reception. Music that is too loud or would be described as obnoxious by most of your guests should be avoided in favor of music that is lighthearted and unobtrusive.

At a Malibu reception in July of 2005, the Bride & Groom's list of background music included mildly upbeat selections from artists like: Jack Johnson, John Mayer, Dave Matthews Band, Coldplay, Ben Harper, Euge Groove, Norah Jones, David Grey, and Keane. As the Meal ended, the guests were having fun and they were ready to start dancing.

> *Bonus Chapters!* As an added special bonus for purchasing this book, you can download 4 free Bonus Chapters. One of them is a detailed list of Background Music Suggestions. Simply register at:
> **TheBestWeddingReceptionEver.com**

The Kissing Couples Drawing ★★★★

It's fairly common at wedding receptions for the guests to clink on their glasses as a signal that they want the Bride & Groom to kiss. You can build on this tradition by adding a fun twist. Provide your MC with a list of several other couples (married, engaged, and dating) that will be in attendance. Then have the MC instruct your guests that each time they tap on their drinking glasses and the two of you kiss, another couple will be randomly selected from the list and called on to stand and kiss while your guests cheer them on. If you are both more outgoing and slightly daring, you could add a fun twist to this idea by requiring that the randomly selected couple kiss first, and then after they have kissed, the two of you must imitate their unique kiss. Soon, your guests will be finding fun and creative ways to make the two of you kiss.

Singing Tables for Kisses ★★★★

Ben Miller, a popular wedding entertainer in Bloomington/Normal, IL, says, *"Try telling your guests that tapping on their drinking glasses to make you kiss just won't work at your reception. Have your MC inform them that as an alternative, if they stand as a table and sing any portion of a song that includes the word "Love," then and only then, will you kiss for them. If your group is already going to be just a little rowdy, soon you may have tables competing to see who can come up with the most creative song."*[1] One creative choice of songs that I have heard on rare occasions is the theme song from the Oscar Mayer® commercial for their bologna. That's right…the word "Love" is in there. This activity is not advisable with a meal that features a buffet or food stations as many guests may not all be seated at the same time. Also, it should be noted that a Live Band may not be able to stop playing when the guests start singing as easily as a DJ or a Wedding Entertainment Director™.

Appoint "Kissing Judges" ★★★★★

This is a humorous option that can be combined with the previous Singing Tables for Kisses idea, the Kissing Couples Drawing, or similar kissing contests. Jim & Denise Sanchez, a wedding entertainment team from Southern California suggest the following: *"Have your MC provide one select table of guests (perhaps one group that is clearly going to be the 'rowdy table') to serve as 'Kissing Judges.' The MC will provide them with large score cards numbered 1-5, just like those used by the judges at ice skating competitions. When the Bride & Groom kiss, the 'Kissing Judges' will raise the score cards and deliver their verdict. If your overall scores are too low, the Bride & Groom (and/or any additional couples) will be called upon to try again and see if they can get a better overall score. Soon, your guests will be trying to make you kiss again, just to see how well the judges will score you. There will undoubtedly be lots of laughter as your guests will cheer you on to a perfect score."*[2]

Singing for Their Dinner ★★★★

This is a fun twist on the previous Singing Tables for Kisses idea that can used with a buffet dinner. When it's time to invite your guests to join the buffet line, ask your MC to instruct your guests that they will not be able to get in the line, until they have serenaded you with a song that includes the word "Love." They will be expected to sing to you as a group in front of your table. Then, and only then, will they be free to get in line for the buffet. Also, it should be noted that a Live Band may not be able to stop playing to accommodate the guests' singing as easily as a DJ or a Wedding Entertainment Director™.

Bride & Groom Buffet Line Trivia ★★★★

When it's time to invite your guests to join the buffet line, Curtis Hoekstra, a popular wedding entertainer in Phoenix, AZ, says, *"Ask your MC to advise your guests that they will be expected to show how much they know about the two of you. They must correctly answer random trivia questions about you, before they can get in the buffet line. To keep too many people from guessing at once, they will need to raise their hand only when they are sure they have the answer. And, if they get the answer wrong, they will have to point to a different table which will be sent to the buffet line ahead of them as a consequence. When done correctly, your guests will be completely entertained while waiting for their turn to go eat."[3]* Also, it should be noted that a Live Band may need to take a break while their MC directs this activity.

Song Titles for Table Names with a Buffet ★★★★★

Name your guests tables based on song titles. The titles can reflect a theme or be used as a "brand" of sorts for the guests at each table. When it's time to invite your guests to join the buffet line, have your MC instruct your guests that they will know they are the next to get in line when their table's corresponding song is played. At a 2005 reception in Silverado Canyon, the Bride & Groom, who had met at a George Strait music festival, named their tables after their favorite George Strait songs.

"Be Our Guest" Catering Staff Introduction ★★★

If the catering staff would like to join in on the fun, have your MC formally announce them into the room while playing "Be Our Guest" from Disney®'s, "Beauty & The Beast®," (or "Hot Hot Hot" by Buster Poindexter). Then, the catering staff will come out and line up, shoulder to shoulder facing your guests, or they might serve the head table their first entrée in dramatic fashion. They might even be carrying plates topped with fancy, silver covers. One location in Orange County, California regularly does this at the beginning of their sit down meals. Check with your caterer and make sure your MC fully understands the music and timing issues involved.

IMPORTANT DISCLAIMERS

1: Some of the ideas presented in this chapter may not fit for you.

2: Don't be afraid to come up with your own creative ideas.

3: It is vital that you discuss with your MC how you want these events to be presented.

4: Make sure you clearly spell out what you consider appropriate and inappropriate.

5: Each MCs level of skill and talent for presenting these events will vary.

6: Ask for video footage to see how your MC actually presents them.

7: Be sure to discuss with your MC how and when you would like to do these events.

The
Meal

Do a Centerpiece Give-Away Activity ★★/★★★★★

If the centerpieces on the guest tables can be taken home as keepsakes, consider using a centerpiece give-away activity to create some fun energy that will leave your guests laughing and/or cheering. These ideas can range from simple to complex, from humorous to energetic, or from generic to highly personalized. They can also serve as ice breakers to help the guests get to know each other at their tables, or just to inject some fun energy into the mealtime. Here are some examples:

Who Has the Winning Chair? ★★/★★★

Place a sticker underneath one chair per table, and then invite your guests to discover who has already won by standing and turning their chairs over in search of the hidden sticker. This can be expanded by having them stand and then rotate around the table, moving from chair to chair as the music plays. When the music suddenly stops, the winner will be revealed by looking under the chair that's currently in front of them. Let your MC know that you want to do this activity and make sure the chairs are not already "labeled" from a previous event. Multiple stickers per table would certainly confuse the guests.

Closest Birthday, Farthest Traveled, Etc. ★★/★★★

Ask the guests to compare specific information about themselves at their own table. Then ask for the one person at each table to stand who has the following: a birthday closest to your wedding date, traveled the furthest, known the Bride & Groom the longest, etc. They could be the winner, or you could ask them to congratulate the person to their right as the winner resulting in a wave of laughter from the guests.

Pennies From Heaven ★★/★★★★★

Put a penny under one bread plate per table, and then invite your guests to lift their bread plates to discover who has already won. For a sit-down meal, be sure to schedule this event to take place before the salad course is completed, as the catering staff will commonly remove the bread plates along with the salad plates. If the MC begins too late, there may no longer be any bread plates to lift up and the pennies will already be in plain view. I share this advice from first hand experience. At a fabulous 2005 reception in New Jersey, I found myself in this exact predicament. With a little ingenuity, I was able to still use the pennies as a trick that convinced most of the guests that they had just magically appeared.

The Napkin Pass ★★★/★★★★★

Have the guests pass a linen napkin around the table, while some music plays, waving it over their heads as it goes. When it stops, the person with the napkin is the winner. Or, they can be asked to fold the napkin and drape it over their left arm as they have now been appointed as their table's waiter and will be responsible for fetching their table's drinks… right after they congratulate the real centerpiece winner on their left.

The Dollar Pass ★★★/★★★★★

Have one person per table volunteer to hold up a one dollar bill which will then be passed around the table as the music plays. When the music stops, the person with the dollar will think they are the winner and they might be if you so choose. But you could tell them that they have won second prize and get to keep the dollar. The person who lost their dollar is now identified as having "purchased" the centerpiece.

Words of Wisdom Cards ★★★★★

Use the Words of Wisdom card idea from page 125 and have the guests fill out one note card each at their tables. Once the cards are completed, have the guests share their answers at their table and then select the one card with the funniest or most creative advice as the winner. The winning cards will then be read aloud by the MC in an entertaining way towards the end of the meal.

First Baby Name Cards ★★★★★

Another twist on the Words of Wisdom Cards is First Baby Name Cards. If neither of you have any children yet, and are planning on starting a family someday and/or the Groom's last name could create some fun suggestions (i.e. Barbee, Dickey, Haze), have the guests fill out one card each at their tables with one fun and creative first baby name. Once the note cards are completed, have the guests share their answers at their table and then select the one card with the funniest or most creative baby name as the winner. The winning cards will then be read aloud by the MC in an entertaining way towards the end of the meal.

A Simple Test for Gauging an MC's Level of Skill & Talent:

You may have noticed that several of the ideas on these two pages have been scored on a sliding scale (i.e. 2-5 stars). These adjustable ratings were created because depending on how skilled and/or knowledgeable your MC is with the added enhancements (i.e. fun elimination twists; creative punch lines; the timing of the punch lines; and/or adding poignant, romantic, and personalization), they may only be able to deliver the simplest version. Use these suggestions as a test. Ask the MC how they are capable of turning these activities into 5 star events. But don't give them all the details. Instead, ask them how they would perform these activities. Their answers may tell you quite a bit about their skill level and knowledge as a wedding entertainer. Also, be sure to request video footage, as the MC may be able to describe it better than they can deliver. This test could help you find the best MC for your reception's entertainment needs.

The
Meal

Your Own Personal "Top 10" List ★★★★★

Randy Bartlett, a nationally known wedding entertainer based out of Sacramento, CA, says, *"Invite your guests to create a David Letterman style 'Top 10' list about the two of you. Have them create 10 fun endings to the line 'The Top 10 Reasons Why Joe & Sally Should Be Together are...' as a table. Then, the best 10 lines from all the tables will be selected, compiled and presented for everyone to hear by the MC at the end of the meal."*[4] It is vital that your MC can compile the best order based on humor, and can confidently deliver the punch lines.

R.S.V.P. Spotlight ★★★★★

Keep track of the first 5 or more guests (i.e. singles, couples, families) to send in their R.S.V.P. and give their names to your MC. Towards the end of the meal, have your MC invite these unwitting guests up to the dance floor to receive some kind of surprise recognition. Playing a mysterious sounding theme in the background can really add to this moment. Then, challenge those in attendance to guess what these people have done to be deserving of whatever honor they are about to receive. As the audience gets involved by throwing out their queries, the MC will finally reveal that the people in question were the most prompt in the room and the first few to send in their R.S.V.P. Then, present them with a small gift, like a box of chocolates or a gift card from Starbucks®, or Blockbuster®.

Future Anniversary Cards ★★★

Place an anniversary card, all with different years of marriage assigned on the envelope, along with a pen on each guest table. Include printed instructions (so the MC won't spoil the surprise by announcing it) that will ask the guests at each table to sign the card, and write a note that you would like them read on that particular anniversary. Once the cards are competed and sealed, they will be collected and put with the regular gift cards, so the bride and groom can discover them later. On many of their anniversaries that follow, the bride and groom will be able to open yet another anniversary card that will bring back fond memories of their wedding day.

Make a Time Capsule ★★★

James Loram, a popular Southern California wedding entertainer, says, *"Place note cards and pens at each table and provide your MC with a small, steel canister to be used as a Time Capsule. Have the MC invite the guests to fill out the cards with their names and some special thoughts they might like to share with the bride and groom. Once the cards have been completed, the MC will collect all of the cards, and any other fun mementos the guests may want to include. These will be sealed inside the steel container until their 1st, 10th, or even 25th anniversary."*[5]

KARL & LORI

October 29th, 2005
Irvine, California

Nobody Danced?

It's quite true...nobody danced at Karl & Lori's Reception. Since neither they, nor their families, would be interested in dancing, they chose to forgo the dance floor and pass on the special dances. However, creating a fun celebration filled with laughter was still a very high priority. So, we planned several unique events to keep their guests fully entertained.

*Newlywed Quiz

We placed Karl & Lori in chairs, seated back to back, and then we quizzed them about how well they really knew each other (i.e. "Which one of you is the better kisser?"). They signaled their answers by holding up a groom's shoe or a bride's shoe, while unable to see the other's response. When they both heartily agreed about which of them had the "crazy family," their guests let out a roar of laughter.

RECEPTION AGENDA

1:00-2:10
Cocktail Hour
"Vocal Jazz Mix"
2:10
Grand Entrance
Wedding Party Themes
"Father Of The Bride Theme"
"Rocky Theme"
"Green Acres Theme"
"Hawaii Five-O Theme"
"The Imperial March"
Love Story Theme
"What A Wonderful World"
by Roger Williams
Bride & Groom's Theme
"Beautiful Day" by U2
2:20
Formal Toasts
2:30
Dinner
Background Music Mix feat.
Glenn Miller, Chris Botti &
Nat King Cole
Salad Course
Kissing Couples Drawing
Longevity Spotlight
"You're Nobody 'Til
Somebody Loves You"
by Dean Martin
3:00
Entrée Course
Centerpiece Give-Away
Words of Wisdom
R.S.V.P. Spotlight
Newlywed Quiz*
3:45
Cake Cutting
"Sweet Happy Life"
by Peggy Lee
"Jaws Theme"
by John Williams
3:55
Chocolate Fountain
4:30
Last Song
"Wonderful Tonight"
by Eric Clapton
Finale Clip
"The Muppet Show
Closing Theme"

KARL & LORI

143

CHAPTER 19

THE SPECIAL DANCES

When your First Dance begins, your guests will certainly be watching. Some will be remembering when they shared their own first dance, years, or even decades earlier. Others might be picturing how they'll look when they finally share their own first dance. But for the two of you, the world may feel like it has suddenly slowed to half speed as you find yourselves lost in each others eyes. The moment is only broken by full smiles and laughter as your husband, that's right he's your husband now, says to you, "Can you believe it? We're really married now!" Unfortunately, some special dances can be given less than special treatment by entertainment vendors who may have long ago forgotten how truly meaningful, personal, and emotional your special dances should be. In this chapter, we will consider several unique ways to turn your special dances into truly meaningful moments that will be unforgettable.

Turn on the Bubble Machine ★★

My grandmother used to make me watch "The Lawrence Welk Show" with her whenever I was visiting. My favorite moment was when the bubbles began to fill the studio's dance floor. But I'm not actually recommending using a bubble machine, even though they provide a dramatic effect. Rather, invite your guests to gather around the dance floor with small bottles of bubbles and invite them to be your bubble machine. Not only will your guests enjoy being more involved in your celebration, but you'll get some really cute photos with bubbles in the air and your smiling guests as the backdrop. When you shop for the bubbles, look for "non-slip" bubbles so your dance floor won't become slippery.

You Light Up My Life ★★★/★★★★★

Ben Miller, a popular wedding entertainer in Bloomington/Normal, IL, says, *"There are high tech and low tech lighting effects that can enhance your First Dance in some truly creative ways. Using specialized lighting, you can dance under a bright spotlight as the room is darkened. You might even choose to have your monogram, or your names, projected in lights that are slowly spinning about the room. Be sure the entertainment vendor you choose has the right equipment and expertise to create these effects properly. For a more low-tech approach, using the guest involvement from the bubble machine idea, provide everyone with sparklers to light and hold as they gather around the dance floor during*

145

your First Dance. Not only will your guests enjoy being more involved in your celebration, but you'll get some striking photos with sparklers glowing all around and your smiling guests as the backdrop. Make sure your MC knows this will be happening so the guests can be reminded ahead of time to get their sparklers ready and lit. Always check this out with your reception location in advance due to possible fire hazard issues. And it's always wise to test your sparklers before buying a large quantity, to see which ones will last the longest and give off the least amount of smoke. Finally, provide 2 or 3 sparklers per guest and have the MC instruct them to use the sparklers only one at a time, so they will last throughout your entire first dance."[1]

Dancing on the Clouds ★★★★★

If bubbles or sparklers are not really your style, perhaps this creative idea suggested by Jorge Lopez, an entertainment production expert from Valencia, CA, will capture your imagination. Jorge says, *"Would you like to create the illusion that the two of you are dancing on top of the clouds? Using the latest in theatrical stage fog technology, combined with specialized lighting effects, an entertainment company with the right tools and qualifications can create this amazing fairytale setting come true."*[2] You can see a video of this effect in action on Jorge's web site: (http://www.uxtm.com/demos/JM/Michele-Angel-wedding.html)[3]. This overall effect is very dramatic, but also very complicated to create. Your entertainment company will need to have a deep understanding about the proper use of the equipment needed to make this effect turn out correctly. It should be noted that this effect shouldn't be attempted with dry ice due to liability issues from slippage.

Rehearse a Choreographed First Dance ★★★★★

For some couples and for many grooms in particular, the prospect of dancing alone in front of your guests for 3 or 4 minutes may be giving you feelings of anxiety. If the mere idea of your fast approaching First Dance is making you nervous, consider the real possibility that some simple dance lessons might actually help you to feel more comfortable and confident. As your comfort and confidence grows during your classes, perhaps you will suddenly find yourself ready to do just a little bit more, like creating and rehearsing your own special, choreographed first dance routine. This can be especially memorable if one, or both, of you are commonly known as non-dancers by your friends and family members. When the music begins and you suddenly put on an amazing show, your guests will not be able to contain their surprise and admiration. And you might just wind up as a star on YouTube.com, like the daring couple featured in this video we'll call, "Wedding First Dance with a Twist": (http://www.youtube.com/watch?v=6qd_j98-y-M&NR)[4]. Their routine was very well rehearsed and highly innovative. It was also plain to hear the impact that it had on their guests. Make sure your MC knows you want to do this and has worked out your music cues.

Record a Special Message ★★★★★

One way to enhance the emotional impact of your special dances is to record a special message that can either precede the song or be mixed into the song during the instrumental segments. If you both were to record messages separately and then have your MC mix them into your First Dance song, it will not only make your dance more personalized and memorable, but it can also be a nice romantic surprise. You will both get to hear the other's words of affection for the very first time on the dance floor. This idea can be added to the other dances as well. One bride in July of 2003 had selected a highly unusual song for her Father/Daughter Dance. When I pressed for more information about the selection, she revealed that when she was little and her dad gave her a bath, he would read books and sing songs to her, and "Joy To The World" by Three Dog Night was one song she remembered most of all. So, whenever she hears that song it would make her think about her father. We recorded her voice giving that explanation, which played over the song's introduction, and brought a tear to her dad's eye, just before he started laughing as the lyrics played over the speakers. Another great example of this creative idea can be seen on Eric & Rebecca's profile featured on page 149. It is very important that your MC fully understands how to do this properly so it won't be presented poorly. The MC will need strong audio editing skills to be able create edits that are both technically superior as well as emotionally powerful. Ask your MC to share some previous examples of special recordings/mixes to gauge their current skill levels in this area.

Wedding Party Dance/Dance Contest ★★★

Turn the typically slow Wedding party dance into a Dance Contest by selecting a fast song that your "entourage" will all enjoy. Then form a circle and see who jumps in the middle to show off their smooth moves. Or, form two lines facing each other, with bridesmaids on one side and groomsmen on the other as they rotate couples down the middle, between the lines, while displaying their best fancy footwork. Some may refer to this as a "Soul Train." This is also commonly referred to as a "Grand March" in the upper Midwest and can easily turn into a snowball dance, or the guests can be invited to join in on the fun part way through.

Invite Others to Join Your Special Dances ★★★

If you are truly uncomfortable sharing your entire First Dance all by yourselves, invite your wedding party members to join in with you after a minute or so. During the Father/Daughter Dance and/or the Mother/Son Dance, your MC could invite any other fathers and daughters, or mothers and sons, who are present to join you on the dance floor. If the Bride has both a Father and a Step-Father, and she has a close relationship with both of them, perhaps her Step-Father could be invited by your MC to "cut in" half way through the Father/Daughter Dance. During your

---

IMPORTANT DISCLAIMERS

1: Some of the ideas presented in this chapter may not fit for you.

2: Don't be afraid to come up with your own creative ideas.

3: It is vital that you discuss with your MC how you want these dances to be presented.

4: Make sure you clearly spell out what you consider appropriate and inappropriate.

5: Each MCs level of skill and talent for presenting these dances will vary.

6: Ask for video footage to see how your MC actually presents them.

7: Be sure to discuss with your MC how and when you would like to do these dances.

8: Make sure your MC knows how to properly pronounce any names that may be challenging.

wedding party dance, your MC could invite the rest of the guests to join in half way through in an effort to lead into the open dancing. Perhaps the MC could invite them up by staggered categories, such as: immediate family, out of state guests, local guests, etc. Make sure your MC knows you would like to invite others to join and knows the timing you would prefer for making such invitations.

The Longevity/Anniversary Dance ★★★★

This special dance creates an opportunity for you to honor, acknowledge, and even seek some free marital advice from the longest married couple in attendance. It can be done a variety of different ways. One method involves inviting all of the married couples to join you for a special dance in honor of marriage. The music starts and during the course of the song the married couples are invited to take their seats based on years of marriage accrued, starting with the two of you and building up towards whoever has been married the longest. As the couples on the dance floor begin to thin out, there will soon be one couple left dancing all by themselves. Your guests will naturally begin to applaud in recognition. At this point, your MC could take a moment to introduce them by name and years of marriage, and maybe even ask them to briefly share their secret for staying married so long. At a 2004 reception in Riverside, the last couple left had been married for 53 years. When I asked them how to stay married for 53 years, the husband's response was, "Don't die!" Because this method does result in an empty dance floor, it might be best to schedule this version to take place just before a slower event, like the Cake Cutting, the Money Dance/Dollar Dance, or the next course of the meal. Another approach is to hold off on starting the song until the longest married couple has first been identified and/or interviewed by simply moving the couples across the dance floor, from one side to the other. Then, once the longest married couple has been revealed, all of the married couples are invited to join them for the entire song, which can create a segue point into your open dancing. After all, your dance floor will most likely already be filled with married couples at this point. If your longest married couple will not be mobile enough to participate, this activity can be done during the meal as a Longevity/Anniversary Spotlight. Between courses or after the buffet line has cleared, have all the couples stand up. Then begin having them sit back down based on years of marriage accrued, starting with the two of you and building up towards whoever has been married the longest. The last couple standing will then be introduced by your MC, and perhaps they'll share their secret for a lasting marriage.

Bonus Chapters! As an added special bonus for purchasing this book, you can download 4 free Bonus Chapters. One of them is a detailed list of Reception Music Suggestions, including some great song ideas for all of your Special Dances. Simply register at:
TheBestWeddingReceptionEver.com

ERIC & REBECCA

January 8th, 2006
Laguna Beach, California

A Mother/Son Dance To Remember

Eric wanted to dance with his Mom to "You Are My Sunshine" because she had taught him to sing the chorus when he was a little boy. His Mother sent me an old cassette that she suggested might help the guests understand why the song was so special to them. The tape had Eric's voice on it, singing the chorus of "You Are My Sunshine" when he was just 3 years old! We made a special edit featuring Eric's adorable little voice singing over the instrumental portion. In the end, they were both surprised and there wasn't a dry eye in sight.

*First Dance

Eric & Rebecca wanted to have fun with their First Dance. So, about a minute into their song, it came to an abrupt halt but immediately transitioned into one of their favorite upbeat numbers. Their guests enjoyed this creative twist.

RECEPTION AGENDA

2:00
Grand Entrance
"Christmas Eve Sarajevo"
by Trans-Siberian Orchestra
2:10
First Dance*
"The Nearness Of You"
by Norah Jones
"I'm On My Way"
By The Proclaimers
2:15-3:20
Toasts & Dinner
Special Dances
Father/Daughter Dance
"The Way You Look Tonight"
by Steve Tyrell
Mother/Son Dance
"You Are My Sunshine"
by Bing Crosby
Parents & Wedding Party
"Through The Eyes Of Love"
By Melissa Manchester
Longevity Dance
"Young At Heart"
by Frank Sinatra
3:20-3:45
Open Dancing
3:45
Cake Cutting
"Knock Me A Kiss"
by Louis Jordan
"I Got You Babe"
by Sonny & Cher
4:00
Bouquet & Garter Toss
"American Woman"
by Lenny Kravitz
"I Need A Man"
By Eurythmics
"I'm A Loser"
By The Beatles
"Minnie The Moocher"
by Big Bad Voodoo Daddy
"Who Let The Dogs Out"
by Baha Men
4:10-4:50
Open Dancing
Last Dance
"True Companion"
by Marc Cohn

ERIC & REBECCA

CHAPTER 20

THE CAKE CUTTING

Dating back to the Roman era, cutting a cake has been a traditional part of wedding celebrations for literally thousands of years. It started as a symbol of fertility, with the husband breaking a wheat cake over his new wife's head to represent that he was ready to start a family with her and was hopeful that she would give him many children. The guests would clamor to eat the falling crumbs, which were believed to bring good luck. In the 16th century, wedding cake began to be served in layers with a delicious frosting. And today, it is commonly seen as your first official meal as husband and wife. Whether you serve each other gently, or give in to your guests' cajoling and treat each other to a face full of frosting, this is one of those moments your guests won't want to miss. In this chapter, we'll look into some fun ways to get your guests a little more involved during your cake cutting and I'll even offer some fun music suggestions.

Have Your Guests Serenade You ★★★★

Your MC can pass out lyric sheets to all of the guests just before your Cake Cutting and then invite everyone to gather around the cake and sing a song to the two of you while you cut your cake and feed each other. There are several great songs that can be lots of fun: "That's Amoré" by Dean Martin, "I Got You Babe" by Sonny & Cher, or "How Sweet It Is (To Be Loved By You)" by Marvin Gaye. If your MC tells your guests this idea is a "surprise" while handing out the lyric sheets, you'll likely get even more participation because everyone likes helping with a fun surprise. Be sure your MC knows that you want to do this, has the lyric sheets ready, and is prepared to help set it up properly.

The Cake Smash with a Sneak Attack ★★★★

Invite your Best Man and Maid/Matron of Honor to join you for a posed picture at the cake to recreate the formal cake cutting photos from the 1940's and earlier. This explanation is merely a ruse that your MC can use to get them into position for what's about to happen next. Just as you're about to feed each other, and your guests are encouraging you to smash the cake, pull a fast one and smash cake on the faces of your Best Man and Maid/Matron of Honor. Your MC and your Photographer should both be informed in advance that you want to do this so they can help you pull it off without your Best Man or Maid/Matron of Honor getting suspicious.

Have the Bridesmaids Pull Cake Charms ★★★★

Cake Charms are small silver charms that are baked into the cake with strings attached. Prior to the cake cutting, these charms can be pulled from the cake by the Bridesmaids, and/or the single ladies in attendance. The charms are supposed to represent what may lie in store for each Bridesmaid who retrieves them. Make sure your MC knows how to properly introduce the significance of the Cake Charms.

Provide a Creative "Groom's Cake" ★★★

In the South and Midwest, it is fairly common to have a "Groom's Cake" in addition to the formal Wedding Cake. Often this cake is chocolate, with chocolate frosting, and decorated with chocolate covered strawberries. However, it is commonly a themed cake, In the movie "Steel Magnolias," the groom's cake was shaped and decorated as an Armadillo. I have seen groom's cakes that were shaped like a surfboard on a wave, a tuxedo, a cowboy boot, etc. At one 2006 reception in Dana Point, the Groom, who was from New York, chose a cake shaped like a Yankees baseball cap. We played some fun Yankees theme music when the cake was presented. Make sure your MC knows you will be having a Groom's cake and is prepared to explain its significance, if necessary.

Honor Someone's Birthday/Anniversary ★★★

If one of your guests in attendance will be celebrating a Birthday or a special Anniversary on your wedding day, have the MC invite them to join you at the cake table so you can present them with the second slice. If it's a Birthday, perhaps you could put a lit candle in the slice of cake and invite everyone to sing "Happy Birthday" to them. Be sure your MC will be aware that this is going to happen and will be prepared to properly introduce them, including correctly pronouncing their names.

Provide "Table Cakes" ★★★

Bill Hermann, a popular wedding entertainer based in Minneapolis, MN, says, *"Have your baker make individual cakes to be set as the centerpieces on each of the guest tables. Before you cut your own smaller, formal cake at the cake table (or on your own table), the MC will ask the guests to select one couple per table who they deem to be the most romantic couple of their group. The MC will then invite each of these "romantic couples" to stand and follow along as the bride and groom are given step by step instructions on their cake cutting process. At the same time, each of the "romantic couples," along with the bride and groom, will cut the cake, serve the first slice onto the plate, feed each other, and then kiss. When they are done, the guests will be invited to cut up and serve their own cakes at each table. Be sure your MC is aware that this is going to happen and will be prepared to properly instruct your guests when the times comes."[1]*

Here Are Some Fun Cake Cutting Music Suggestions:

"Cut The Cake" *by The Average White Band*

"Don't Be Cruel" *by Elvis Presley*

"Don't Be Cruel" *by Cheap Trick*

"Grow Old With Me" *by John Lennon*

"Grow Old With You" *by Adam Sandler*

"Hit Me With Your Best Shot" *by Pat Benatar*

"Honeysuckle Rose" *by Louis Armstrong & Velma Middleton*

"How Sweet It Is (To Be Loved By You)" *by Marvin Gaye*

"How Sweet It Is (To Be Loved By You)" *by James Taylor*

"Ice Cream" *by Sarah McLachlan*

"I Got You Babe" *by Sonny & Cher*

"I Got You Babe" *by UB40 with Chrissie Hynde*

"Jaws Theme" *by John Williams*

"Knock Me A Kiss" *by Louis Jordan*

"Love And Marriage" *by Frank Sinatra*

"Mack The Knife" *by Bobby Darin*

"Pour Some Sugar On Me" *by Def Leppard*

"Recipe For Love" *by Harry Connick, Jr.*

"Sleepwalk" *by Johnny & Santo*

"Sleepwalk" *by Larry Carlton*

"Somewhere In Time Theme" *by Roger Williams*

"St. Elmo's Fire: Love Theme" *by David Foster*

"Sugar, Sugar" *by The Archies*

"Sweet Happy Life" *by Peggy Lee*

"That's Amoré" *by Dean Martin*

"Whatever Will Be, Will Be (Que Sera)" *by Doris Day*

"When I'm Sixty-Four" *by The Beatles*

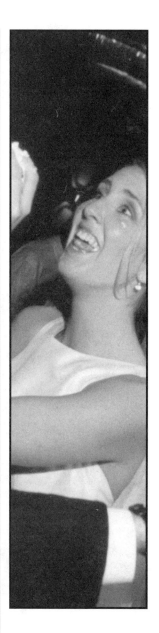

*Bonus Chapters! As an added special bonus for purchasing this book, you can download 4 free Bonus Chapters. One of them is a detailed list of Reception Music Suggestions. The list above is a sample of the great song ideas that are included. Simply register at:

TheBestWeddingReceptionEver.com

The
Cake
Cutting

CHAPTER 21

THE MONEY DANCE/DOLLAR DANCE

Some brides have been known to spend upwards of $10,000 or more for a Vera Wang bridal gown. Most grooms will typically only spend $120 to rent their tuxedo. Decorative floral centerpieces for twenty guest tables can easily average $500 or more. But what's the value of giving your guests a chance to dance and connect with you, one on one, during your wedding reception? Some would say...PRICELESS! The most common misperception about the Money Dance/Dollar Dance is that your guests will only see it as the two of you begging for honeymoon spending cash. However, in my experience, that couldn't be further from the truth. If you are truly uncomfortable with this event, then don't do it. But in this chapter, we will discuss a few ways to make it more enjoyable, including some alternate options that remove the references to money altogether.

Regulate the Lines ★★★

If you have a large guest count (200 or more), your Money Dance could drag on far longer than desirable and start to have a negative impact on the success of your reception celebration. If your Best Man and Maid/Matron of Honor are willing to pitch in and help you regulate the lines of people who are waiting for their turn to dance with you, they can send the guests to cut in more frequently then they might have been inclined to do all on their own. Sending in a new person every 45 seconds or even sooner can keep things moving at a steady pace. Be sure your MC knows this will be happening, so instructions on the timing can be given to your Best Man and Maid/Matron of Honor.

Bring Safety Pins for the Groom ★★

When guests come up to dance with the groom, they'll be given safety pins so can they pin their greenbacks all over his tuxedo. Pretty soon the groom will be covered with cash, literally. Make sure your MC knows that safety pins will be used so the guests can be informed.

Bring Your Own Creative "Purse" ★

White, satin purses for this event can be commonly found at bridal shops. But don't be afraid to come up with your own creative "purse." Your Maid/Matron of Honor can hold a treasure chest or a large tip jar. Or, bring an old white pillow case with a big dollar sign ($) printed on it.

Don't Call It a Money Dance/Dollar Dance ★★★★

If the idea of a Money Dance/Dollar Dance makes you uncomfortable, but the underlying purpose of connecting with your guests, one on one, is causing an internal conflict, try removing the money aspect of this event from the equation. You don't have to call it a Money Dance/Dollar Dance. You can give it any name you want. Call it a Special Dance, a Honeymoon Dance, a Congratulatory Dance, etc. Have your MC announce it with no mention of the word "money" while instead putting the focus on how this will be an opportunity for your guests to offer their best wishes to you, one on one. Truth be told, even without mentioning the word money, I have seen several of these "Special Dances" where a fair amount of the guests still came up with money in hand. But the bride and groom were no longer uncomfortable because there had been no overt request for money. It is very important that your MC understands your wishes in this regard. Some MCs have a habit of making the same announcements at every wedding the same exact way, as if they are on autopilot. If the MC is not clear on your preferences, then a canned introduction that includes references to money could still happen.

Run with the "Money Theme" ★★★★

If doing a Money Dance/Dollar Dance is not only a comfortable idea for you, but may be something you've actually been looking forward to, why not try having some fun with it? Instead of worrying about what your guests will think, have your MC invite them to bring up 10's, 20's, and all major credit cards. Play "Money Themed" musical selections and instruct the guests that they must dance with you in a style that matches the tempo of each song. Put a fundraiser thermometer on the wall with an outrageously high projected goal for the night. Ask your MC to use your honeymoon destination along with a bad impression of a televangelist to make a plea for funds that sounds something like this:

"Brothers and Sisters-uh, I've had vision from God-uh of these two lovely children enjoying a beautiful honeymoon-uh on the beaches of Hawaii-uh. But I'm sad to tell you that vision-uh will not become a reality-uh unless you are willing-uh to open up your purse strings-uh and give-uh. So right now-uh, I'm asking you-uh...I'm pleading with you-uh...to dig deep Brothers and Sisters-uh, so we can make sure this vision-uh become a reality-uh. They can accept all denominations-uh, and out of state checks-uh. And they'll even be more happy-uh to take your credit cards-uh."

Now, I know that example was completely over the top. But you might be surprised to know that I actually used it back in 1997 at the specific request of a bride and groom who wanted to do something that was...completely over the top. That was their style. It fit them perfectly. What's your style? Be very clear with your MC about how you might want to run with the "Money Theme" at your reception. Be sure they can present your ideas appropriately as well.

The Dollar Pass Jump Start ★★★★

Building on the Dollar Pass idea from page 141, Ron Ruth, a popular wedding entertainer from Kansas City, MO, says, *"To get past the initial lull that can occur as we are waiting for the guests to begin forming lines for the Money Dance/Dollar Dance, why not use the Dollar Pass idea as a fun way to segue into this event that will be both entertaining and surprising. When the Dollar Pass event ends, the MC will instruct those that have been left holding the dollar to bring it with them to the dance floor, as they have been selected for a special honor. The MC will guide the men and women to form into separate lines along the edge of the dance floor. Then, the bride and groom will be invited up to the dance floor as the rest of the guests will finally be told that this is indeed the Money Dance/Dollar Dance and they are all invited to get into either of the lines and participate."*[1]

The Polka Money Dance/Dollar Dance ★★★★★

Bill Hermann, a popular wedding entertainer based in Minneapolis, MN, says, *"Instead of playing the typical slow or medium speed songs during the Money Dance/Dollar Dance, have the entertainment vendors play a series of upbeat Polkas. Then, have the bride's father and groom's father regulate the lines, while exchanging the guest's larger bills for brand new one dollar bills. Instruct the guests to throw their wad of bills into the air above the bride and groom as they are sent out to cut in. Soon there will be dollar bills flying everywhere and more of your guests will not only want to participate, but they'll bring larger bills to exchange for singles giving them the opportunity to make a larger 'cash confetti' explosion over you than the previous person."*[2]

The Money Dance/Dollar Dance Dunk Tank ★★★★★

Bill Hermann has also offered the following suggestion for an outdoor reception. *"If the bride and groom are into baseball or softball, bring in a dunk tank and get the groomsmen to volunteer to strip down to swim trunks and t-shirts. The guests will be given 1 ball to throw at the dunk tank for every dollar they give during the Money Dance/Dollar Dance."*[3]

Words of Wisdom Cards Instead of Cash ★★★★

Ben Miller, a popular wedding entertainer in Bloomington/Normal, IL, says, *"If you'd prefer not ask your guests for money, but you still want to connect with them in the manner provided by a Money Dance/Dollar Dance, have your guests fill out note cards with their names on one side and their best Words of Wisdom for achieving a long and happy marriage. Then, instead of bringing money in exchange for a dance, they will give you their Words of Wisdom cards and you'll have a great keepsake to take with you and read on your honeymoon."*[4]

"Play 'Money Themed' musical selections and instruct the guests that they must dance with you in a style that matches the tempo of each song."

The Money/Dollar Dance

157

CHAPTER 22

THE BOUQUET & GARTER TOSS

Who among your single guests will be the ones getting married next? Finding the answer to this question has been the underlying purpose of the Bouquet & Garter Toss events for quite a long time. Nowhere are the stark differences between men and women more apparent than during these events. The single ladies, more often than not, are eager and excited to participate. Not just because they may already be hoping to get married soon, but also because the thought of catching something that belonged to the bride on her wedding day can be excitement enough. The single men, more often than not, come up begrudgingly and can be seen with their hands in their pockets or holding a beer, thus limiting their chances to catch the garter. On some rare occasions the gathered group of bachelors, have been seen parting as if the garter was Moses and they were the Red Sea. The flying garter then falls towards the dance floor with nary a hand reaching out to stop its descent. In this chapter, we'll delve into some creative twists that can make these events more memorable, including some ideas that will actually make the single guys want to scramble for the flying garter!

The Teddy Bear Toss ★★★

Greg Lowder, a popular wedding entertainer in Seattle, WA, suggests, *"If you will have several small children in attendance who might feel left out of the Bouquet & Garter Toss events try holding a separate toss event for the kids, before the "full size" toss events. Toss a teddy bear or a large stuffed animal and take a photo with the child who catches it."*[1]

The Bouquet Presentation ★★★

If you will have a limited number of single ladies in attendance, or perhaps you would just prefer not to put them on the spot, why not do a Bouquet Presentation to someone you appreciate? Perhaps a newly engaged female friend. Maybe even the longest married couple?

The MIRV Bouquet Toss ★★★

If you are worried that only tossing one bouquet will cause others to feel left out, why not toss a bouquet that breaks into 4 or 5 smaller bouquets in flight? (MIRV refers to a missile that has multiple warheads.)

Involve the Married People Instead ★★★★

If you have a limited number of single friends in attendance, but still want to present your bouquet and garter to someone, try this creative suggestion submitted by Randy Bartlett, a nationally known wedding entertainer based out of Sacramento, CA. *"Bring all the married ladies up to one corner of the dance floor. Have them cross to the opposite corner (where the bride is standing) by ascending years of marriage. Upon revealing the identity of the longest married woman, have the bride present her with the toss bouquet. Repeat this process with the married men, but call them over to the groom in descending years of marriage to reveal the man who has been married the shortest amount of time. Have the groom present him with the garter."*[2]

Bouquet & Garter Switch ★★★

Pull a fast one by arranging for your MC to stop the music just before the Bouquet Toss is about to occur. The bride will then drag the groom out and seat him a chair as she begins pulling up his pant leg while some sexy music is playing. The guests will hoot and holler when it's revealed that the groom is wearing the garter. The bride removes and tosses it to the single ladies. Then the groom tosses the bouquet to the single men.

Don't Stop the Dancing ★★★

If the dancing is going strong and everyone is having fun, why bring it to a halt just to toss the bouquet and garter? Instead, why not have the bride and groom do the tosses from the fully packed dance floor? The MC can instruct the single ladies and single guys to raise their hands, or you can let go of that tradition and make it fair game for anyone to catch them.

Make Him Dance First ★★★

Before the bride will let the groom remove her garter, the MC will instruct the groom that he must put on a sexy dance for her first. Only when she finally gives him the "go ahead" wave will he finally be allowed to start removing the garter.

Skip the Garter Removal ★★★

If you, or your guests, might be more conservative, and the removal of the garter may be perceived as too racy, just skip it. Have the groom produce the garter from a pocket. Or, the bride can simply hand it to him. Then, proceed with the garter toss event as you see fit.

The Best Man/"Human Chair" ★★★

Ask the best man to serve as a "human chair" for the bride to sit upon while the groom removes the garter. The best man can "get down on all fours" while the bride sits on his back, of he can get down on one knee while the bride is seated on his other leg.

The Handcuffed Groom ★★★

Have the best man put the groom in handcuffs before the garter removal begins, with his hands behind his back so he can't use his hands to remove the garter. Your entertainment vendors can play "Bad Boys" by Inner Circle (the TV show theme for "Cops") to really set the mood.

The "Mary Poppins" Trick ★★★

In the movie "Mary Poppins," the main character astounds the children in her care by pulling oversized items out of her satchel. Have the bride sit on chair that has a cloth chair cover on it. Place the chair with its back to a table that is covered with a table cloth. Then, have an accomplice feed oversized items to the groom from under the table and the chair, One couple who actually suggested this idea had the groom withdraw several oversized items from underneath the bride's dress during the garter removal, including: golf clubs, a carnival sized stuffed animal, and tall lamp. The guests could hardly contain themselves.

The "Star Trek" Removal ★★★/★★★★★

If both of you are star trek fans, have the groom enter the room wearing the classic James T. Kirk, gold, spandex top. Play the original "Star Trek" TV show theme while the groom lip syncs to William Shatner's voice saying, *"...to boldly go where no man has gone before!"* After which the groom can take out his "tricorder" and begin taking readings while removing the garter. If your friends already know that you are both sci-fi geeks, blow their minds by proudly embracing the label.

The "Mission: Impossible" Removal ★★★/★★★★★

Alexander Tamas, a popular wedding entertainer and professional MC based in Victoria, B.C. in Canada, says, *"Why not try creating a fun, scripted introduction for the groom (in the style of the TV show, 'Mission: Impossible') which can be presented by the MC while the show's theme song is playing. Make something up about the garter containing a hidden microchip with information on it that could end civilization as we know it. You could even include a warning that the device is booby trapped to go off when touched by human skin, thus requiring the groom to use his teeth."*[3]

The Spelunker's Removal ★★★

One couple, in July of 2003, who were both avid spelunker's (cave explorers), decided to work that into their garter removal in a creative way. The groom put on a head-mounted flashlight commonly used by

<table>
<tr><td>

IMPORTANT DISCLAIMERS

1: Some of the ideas presented in this chapter may not fit for you.

2: Don't be afraid to come up with your own creative ideas.

3: It is vital that you discuss with your MC how you want these events to be presented.

4: Make sure you clearly spell out what you consider appropriate and inappropriate.

5: Each MCs level of skill and talent for presenting these events will vary.

6: Ask for video footage to see how your MC actually presents them.

7: Be sure to discuss with your MC how and when you would like to do these events.

</td></tr>
</table>

The Bouquet & Garter Toss

spelunker's before proceeding to dig under the bride's dress for the elusive garter. Their friends and family got a big kick out this idea.

The NFL Themed Garter Toss ★★★/★★★★★

After the groom has successfully removed the garter, have the MC bring out a small football with a large marker so the bride and groom can autograph it and put their wedding date on it. While the "NFL Theme" or "Monday Night Football Theme" is playing, let the groom toss the ball over the heads of the waiting bachelors. They will fight and scramble to catch the football like its game day. If the MC can deliver a scripted narration in the style of the NFL Films (*"On any given Sunday..."*), this event can really become 5 star. This idea can be personalized a variety of different ways. The small football can be from the groom's favorite team. Use a favorite college fight song along with a small football from that college. Use an oversized stuffed baseball, a mini basketball, etc.

The Garter Toss with a Bribe ★★★

Use a safety pin to attach a 20 dollar bill to the garter. Play the theme song from the popular TV show, "The Apprentice" ("For The Love Of Money" by the O'Jays) to build the energy. Watch as the single men push and shove each other as they try to catch the garter...and the cash!

The Garter Placement with a Switch ★★★★

One idea that is overdone, and can be highly uncomfortable for the participants, is the "tradition" of having the man who caught the garter place it on the leg of the lady who caught the bouquet (This is more commonly done at weddings on the East Coast). However, this idea can create some good laughs if the man is blindfolded and the single lady's leg is then secretly replaced with the groom's hairy leg.

Pick Your Own Music for Each Moment ★★★

I once coached a DJ who played "You Can Leave Your Hat On" by Joe Cocker for the garter toss event. When we were discussing his performance afterwards, I pointed out how that song really fit for the moment when the groom was removing the garter, but it didn't fit the introduction, when all the single men were being gathered, or the moment of the toss when they were supposed to be competing to catch the garter. Feel free to pick out at least 2 songs for the bouquet (Intro & Toss) and 3 or more for the garter (Intro, Removal, & Toss).

Bonus Chapters! As an added special bonus for purchasing this book, you can download 4 free Bonus Chapters. One of them is a detailed list of Reception Music Suggestions, including over 70 great song ideas for the Bouquet & Garter Toss events. Simply register at:
TheBestWeddingReceptionEver.com

CURTIS & AMY

March 4th, 2005
Scottsdale, Arizona

RECEPTION AGENDA

5:30-6:40
Drinks & Appetizers
6:40
Grand Entrance
"The Way You Move"
by OutKast
6:50
First Dance
"My Love"
by Lionel Richie
7:00-7:45
Dinner*
7:45
Toasts
8:00-8:30
Open Dancing
8:30
Cake Cutting
"I Can't Help Myself"
by Four Tops
"Sugar, Sugar"
by The Archies
8:45-9:00
Money Dance
9:00-10:25
Open Dancing
9:20-9:30
Bouquet & Garter Toss
"Lady Marmalade"
from Moulin Rouge Sdtk
"Play That Funky Music"
by Wild Cherry
10:25
Last Dance
"At Last"
by Etta James
"Someone Like You"
by Van Morrison
"Let's Get It On"
by Marvin Gaye

The Return of The Damooko Brothers!

Long before Curtis & Amy first met, Curtis and his buddies used to go out to the nightclubs dressed up and in character as the fictional, infamous "Damooko Brothers". Just for fun, during the Garter Removal and Toss, the "Damooko Brothers" made one more public appearance, much to the joy and satisfaction of the ladies in attendance, including Amy.

*Dinner

Curtis & Amy chose a Buffet dinner service and they selected table names based on fun song titles that matched the people seated there. (i.e. Amy's family was seated at the "We Are Family" table) The guests were told to wait until their table song was playing before they could go get in the line. When a table finally heard their song, many of them sang and danced their way over to the buffet line.

CHAPTER 23

OTHER SPECIAL TOUCHES

When your guests attend your wedding receptions, they do so because they care about you, they support you, they want to congratulate you, and they want to celebrate with you. The most successfully entertaining receptions are the ones where your guests are invited to connect with you and each other in fun, meaningful, and memorable ways. One major reason why guests will leave a reception early is because they are not enjoying themselves. If your friends and family members are overlooked during your reception, they will feel like they are only observers of your festivities. But when they are given an opportunity to connect, they will feel like highly valued contributors. And after all, isn't that the reason you invited them to your wedding reception in the first place? In this chapter, we'll delve into a plethora of ideas that help you to build stronger connections at your celebration with the people who have already made such valuable contributions to both your lives.

The Family Unity Candle ★★★★★

Jim & Denise Sanchez, a wedding entertainment team from Southern California, suggested the following: *"If you haven't already done a Unity Candle in your Ceremony, consider providing for a Family Unity Candle to be set up on your head table or sweetheart table. Ask your MC to inform your guests about the symbolism of the Family Unity Candle representing that when your guests first arrived they were two separate families. But now that you are married, they will be celebrating together as one big happy family. The MC will then invite someone to represent both families by coming up and lighting the outer candles. This can be anyone you choose, such as: your mothers, both set of parents, or someone in your family who hasn't yet been included. The guests will then be instructed about their role. When the bride and groom make their grand entrance, and after the applause is dying down, they will take the outside lit candles and light the center candle representing the uniting of both families into one. At that moment, everyone will begin to applaud and cheer to show their support."*[1]

Messages from the "Best Wishes" Hotline ★★★★

If you have friends and loved ones who will not be able to attend your reception, set up a "Best Wishes" Hotline! If your MC or entertainment vendors are prepared to help, perhaps they will let you use their business

phone line and answering machine, after business hours, so your guests that are unable to attend can call in and leave their own "Best Wishes" messages for the two of you. It would be best to let your MC edit the messages for length and impact as you really shouldn't be privy to the contents of these messages before they are presented. Then the best portions of these messages will be played for all the guests to hear after the toasts or towards the end of the meal. This would be a good moment to capture on video as well, so your loved ones, who participated via telephone, can have a chance to see what your reactions were when their message was played.

Have a Coloring Contest for the Kids ★★★

Building on the Circle of Love idea, Randy Bartlett, a nationally known wedding entertainer based out of Sacramento, CA, says, *"If you have several small children in attendance, bring some coloring books and a few boxes of crayons. Have your MC help them get started in a coloring contest. Don't forget to provide a small prize for all the participants."* [2]

Have Someone Perform a Song ★★★★

If you have a friend who is musically talented, perhaps you might want them to perform a song or two at your reception. Maybe they could even provide the music and singing for your First Dance. Or maybe you, yourself, are a musician and/or a singer. Take a moment towards the end of the meal, or maybe after the cake cutting, to perform a song or two. Your new spouse will love it and your guests will certainly enjoy it as well. Make sure to arrange any special needs for amplifying your instruments, or securing instrumental accompaniment tracks for your performance, with your MC ahead of time.

Sorority Song for the Bride ★★★

If you, the bride, are a member of a college Sorority, and it is traditional for your Sorority sisters to serenade you with a special song at your reception, work with your MC to place it into your agenda. This event can serve as a great lead in for the Bouquet Toss.

Put on a Choreographed Dance Routine ★★★★

At a 1999 reception in Santa Ana, CA, the bride came up with a creative idea that really set the mood for their open dancing. She and her bridesmaids had been rehearsing a choreographed dance routine to a song from the "Grease" soundtrack and they were looking forward to putting on a show for the groom as a surprise. After placing this into the agenda right before the open dancing, I suggested to her that it might be even more fun to follow up their performance by asking the groom and his groomsmen to put on their own choreographed routine in response. Knowing her groom and his groomsmen really well, I knew they would jump at this chance. But, the catch was, they were not going to find out until the moment we announced it, following the show put on by the ladies. As the bride and her bridesmaids finished their routine and the crowd was responding with waves of applause, we announced that it was now the groom's turn as I handed him a hard hat and invited his groomsmen to come help out. They were completely caught off guard! But as soon as "Macho Man" by Village People began to play, they instantly began performing their own completely unrehearsed dance routine. When they finished, the crowd was cheering and giving all of them, bridesmaids and groomsmen, a standing ovation. Needless to say, getting everyone dancing was a pretty easy task after that.

At a Newport Beach reception in 2000, the groom was in a wheelchair. He and his bride opted not to do a first dance as a result. When I spoke with the bride privately, I suggested that she might want to consider enlisting the help of her bridesmaids in creating a fun, choreographed dance routine as a creative replacement for her first dance. When the time came, we sat the groom on the edge of the dance floor as his bride and her bridesmaids put on a creative routine inspired by the opening credits for the movie, "My Best Friend's Wedding." The song they used was "Wishin' And Hopin'" by Ani Difranco. Their dance routine was a complete surprise for the groom and the guests, and it ended with the bride falling, as if swooning, into the groom's lap. Everyone loved it.

There are no limits to how fun and creative these ideas can be. Let your imagination be your guide. Keep in mind that your guests are hoping to have an entertaining time at your reception, but when you provide some of the entertainment yourselves in an unexpected and creative way, your guests will get even more excited about helping you celebrate. If you would enjoy seeing different examples of how a crowd will react to a routine like this, check out these recent videos posted on YouTube.com. The first link, which we'll call, "Wedding Party Thriller", is a homage to Michael Jackson's infamous music video featuring undead dancers, "Thriller": (http://www.youtube.com/watch?v=OPmYbP0F4Zw&eurl=)[3] The second link features a completely unique routine, presented by the bride's father and brothers, which we'll call, "Dance For My Sister's Wedding": (http://www.youtube.com/watch?v=uojhahf7lo4)[4] If you choose to do any routines of this nature, be sure your MC knows how you want it introduced and is prepared for your music cues.

The Toilet Paper Race ★★

This is a silly game that makes a big mess in an effort to determine whether the bride or groom will be the one who will "call the shots," "wear the pants," or "control the checkbook" in your marriage relationship. Your best man and maid/matron of honor are instructed to each place their index fingers into a roll of toilet paper as the bride and groom will be challenged to unravel their roll the fastest. The guests will cheer them on as toilet paper goes flying everywhere.

The Newlywed Quiz ★★★★★

Andy Austin, a popular wedding entertainer from Dallas/Forth Worth, TX, says, *"Letting your guests have a good laugh at your expense can be a great way to liven things up just before kicking off the open dancing. The MC will seat the bride and groom in chairs, back to back, preferably on the dance floor so your guests can see what's about to happen. The bride and groom will both be given objects to hold that will represent both of them, one in each hand. You can use bridal themed Barbie and Ken dolls, small signs on a stick that have "bride" and "groom" (or your first names) printed on them, an empty wine bottle for the bride and an empty beer bottle for the groom, or the bride and groom can remove their shoes, and trade one apiece. The MC will then ask the bride and groom a series of pointed questions to see how well they really know each other. The questions must be precisely worded so that the only answers given are "the bride" or "the groom." When questions like, "Which one of you is the better kisser?" and "Who is better with money?" are posed, the bride and groom will both respond candidly, without saying a word, by simply raising whichever object represents their answer. As they are seated back to back, they are unable to see each other's replies, which can result in some great reactions from the guests. A good MC will also be ready to ad-lib in response to any particularly funny moments as they occur."[5]*

The "Love Story" Presentation ★★★★★

This creative performance piece was submitted by Mark & Rebecca Ferrell, a nationally known wedding entertainment team and recognized performance trainers from Temecula, CA. *"Wedding Receptions are a celebration of love. The love you both share for each other, and the love you, and your friends and family, share as well. Because guests can get easily distracted, it can be common for them to lose sight of how important your reception really is for the two of you. After seeing guests not paying attention during the first dance at weddings, Rebecca and I developed the concept of the "Love Story" as an event that could serve to reacquire your guests' focus and attention where it belonged during your first dance, on the bride and groom. We also found that by dramatically re-telling the story of how you met and fell in love, your guests felt even more connected to you both. By gathering information from the two of you separately, and then combining them into an engaging "love story" presentation, your guests will find themselves participating in the drama as we take them into humorous moments resulting in laughter and poignantly touching moments that may draw out some emotional tears. When your story has ended and your first dance begins, all eyes will be on the two of you and everyone will realize just how lucky you both are to have found each other. This is not just an MC reading a script. It is an emotionally moving performance piece that requires an amazing amount of talent, skill and training to deliver effectively. When done correctly, your guests will remember it for years to come. When done poorly, the results can be embarrassing and even downright painful. It is imperative that you choose only the very best, proven entertainer. Ask to see video of their previous "love story" presentations and ask about their performance background and/or training."*[6] It should also be noted here that Mark & Rebecca Ferrell have trained talented wedding entertainers across the United States, and internationally, in performance based workshops designed to help these entertainers present this "love story" concept as powerfully and effectively as possible. It might be worth your time to contact Mark & Rebecca Ferrell for a list of entertainers who have participated in their training workshops. Mark & Rebecca Ferrell were also among the first to open my eyes to many of the concepts that have been shared in this book.

The Video Montage ★★★

If you decide to create a video montage to show at your reception, here are a few guidelines and ideas you may want to consider and/or include. A good video montage that runs too long is no longer a good video montage. One bride's father at a wedding in August of 2000 wanted to show a video he had put together that was a full hour in length. Instead, it was played during the rehearsal dinner. A good time frame to consider for the total duration of a video montage is under 10 minutes. If you arranged for someone to videotape your proposal, that would be great footage to include in your montage. Using a short segment of photos to honor departed loved ones can be a measured way to keep the mood from coming down, while still recognizing their impact in your life. Be sure your videographer and MC can run a test of the montage before the reception begins in case any troubleshooting may be needed.

The "Instant Edit" Video Montage ★★★★★

Carl Young, a highly talented, professional wedding videographer based in Southern California, says, *"If you want to make your video montage into something really remarkable, try upgrading your video package to include a 'Instant Edit' Video Montage. Your guests will be amazed when they see actual live footage from your Ceremony and your Grand Entrance included in your montage at the end of the meal! It's not easy or cheap, but the effect it will have on your guests will be amazing."*[7]

The "Instant Edit" Photo/Video Montage ★★★★★

Building on the "Instant Edit" Video Montage idea, Mike Colón, a nationally known wedding photographer and sought after photography coach, says, *"While your guests are enjoying their cake, why not give them (and yourselves) a sneak preview of your photo album? Using the latest in wireless technology, my assistant can begin prepping your photos just moments after I've captured them. A short montage of the best shots can then be shown set to your favorite music."*[8] I was lucky enough to see one of these "Instant Edit" videos with Mike at a reception in July of 2004. The guests completely loved it!

CHAPTER 24

THE OPEN DANCING

You may find this hard to believe, but if the rest of the advice given in this book has been taken into consideration, along with the creative ideas discussed in the previous 10 chapters, getting your guests to participate during the dancing won't be difficult at all. Your dance floor will be the natural destination where your guests will arrive because they will want to keep celebrating with you. If they have been having an enjoyable time, the reception has been flowing smoothly, and they've been included and engaged in the festivities from the very beginning, there will be no need for the guilt-trip tactics and the force-fed dance routines that have played such a large part in creating the overall negative public perceptions about wedding entertainers. However, every crowd is different. Being prepared to jump-start your open dancing, if needed, can serve as added insurance that your guests will dance. In this chapter, we'll expose some of the best kept secrets wedding entertainers have used to kick off lively dancing in a lighthearted and engaging manner.

Start Off Slow ★★★

One of the simplest methods for attracting people to an empty dance floor is to simply lower the lighting and play a well known romantic ballad, like "Unchained Melody" by The Righteous Brothers. People dance to music they know. At a wedding reception, there will be no shortage of couples who would love to share a dance during a romantic slow song. This simple idea can also be used to recover from a dance floor that has suddenly cleared, due to an undesirable genre change.

Group Photo on the Dance Floor ★★★★

If your photographer is already planning on taking a group photo of you with all of your guests, why not set up the shot on the dance floor just before the dancing is set to begin? Some, who might not otherwise step foot on the dance floor, will gladly come up to participate with you in taking a large group photo. Have the entertainment vendors play some fun, upbeat music to start warming up the crowd as they are getting ready to pose. "Freeze Frame" by J. Geils Band and "Photograph" by Def Leppard are two fun songs that might fit for this moment. The MC will make sure the guests can hear the photographer's instructions for the photos over the music. Then when the photos are done, the dance music will begin right away as the MC invites everyone to get involved.

The Group Hug Kick Off ★★★★

Have your MC invite your parents to come hold hands in a tight circle around the two of you in the center of the dance floor. Next, the MC will invite the wedding party to do the same in a slightly larger circle around the parents. Then invite the immediate family on the bride's side followed by the groom's immediate family to follow the pattern. Soon the out of town guests will be invited up followed by the local guests. Now, all of your guests will be surrounding you in concentric circles on the dance floor. There are a few different options from here. The MC could encourage the guests to squeeze into the center so they can all give you one big group hug. Once they are all packed in close, the MC will ask the bride to raise her hands so everyone can see her. At that point the MC will identify the bride as the leader and begin a Conga line song, like "Conga" by Gloria Estefan or "Hot Hot Hot" by Buster Poindexter as the MC tells the guests to grab someone else's shoulders and get in the line. If the bride makes her way through the tables and then back to dance floor, a large portion of your guests will keep dancing from that point forward. Another direction that could be taken by the MC would be to start a few circle oriented group songs like: "New York, New York" by Frank Sinatra, "The Hokey Pokey" by Ray Anthony, or even a rendition of "The Chicken Dance." Granted, some of these songs have been truly overdone at wedding receptions, but this is your celebration. If you and your families like doing "The Hokey Pokey" or "The Chicken Dance," by all means make them a fun part of your "must play" dancing requests.

The Shoulder Rub/Conga Line ★★★★

When its time to get the dancing started, your MC will invite the guests to stand and place their right hip on the back of their chair. Since they have all been sitting for awhile, they will then be asked to reach forward and massage the shoulders of the person in front of them so everyone can get nice and relaxed. Then the MC will start a Conga line song, like "Conga" by Gloria Estefan or "Hot Hot Hot" by Buster Poindexter as the guests will be told to keep their hands on the shoulders in front of them and link up with the other tables on their way to the dance floor. Soon, the entire room is participating in a Conga line dance that will wrap up back on the dance floor leading into the rest of the open dancing.

The Snowball Dance ★★★

The Snowball Dance can be used to quickly jumpstart your open dancing during the Wedding Party Dance. The MC will give instructions that when the word "Snowball!" is announced, whoever is currently on the dance floor will be required to instantly go find another person to dance with amongst the guests who are still seated. The guests are instructed that they have to comply when approached by one of the dancers. After just a few calls of "Snowball!" your dance floor will soon be packed with the majority of your guests.

The Torpedo Dance ★★★★

Bill James McElree, a popular wedding entertainer and bridal show producer in the Great White North of Sudbury, Ontario in Canada, says, *"Building on the Snowball Dance idea, why not try something that is a bit more directed and engaging, known as the Torpedo Dance. Just as the Wedding Party Dance can turn into a Snowball Dance, the MC will instruct the guests that whenever the word "Torpedo" is used along with a physical location in the room directed by the MC, those on the dance floor will rush to the directed location and drag more dancers back with them to the dance floor. You can torpedo individual tables randomly around the room until the dance floor begins to fill. Then you can torpedo small sections of the room followed by one half of the room and then the other. Soon, your entire dance floor is packed and everyone is having a great time in the process."*[1]

The Chicken Dance/Fertility Dance ★★★★

At a June 2005 reception in West Covina, the bride's mother had insisted that we play "The Chicken Dance" sometime during the night. After the general festivities were completed and it was time to resume the open dancing, we called the bride's father and mother out to the center of the dance floor and asked the rest of the guests to form one large circle, holding hands around the outside edge of the dance floor. Knowing that some of the guests might not have joined in if we had announced it as "The Chicken Dance," we used a fun ruse to get them involved instead. We shared that the bride's parents were thrilled to celebrate their daughter's wedding, but they were also hopeful that someday soon they might be able to call themselves grandparents. So, with the help of their friends and family, we told them that we were all about to do an ancient fertility dance. The guests began to groan and laugh when they heard "The Chicken Dance " begin to play, but they all danced and had fun too.

SOME HELPFUL SUGGESTIONS
1: Your MC should be consulted if you want to use one of these ideas to jump start your open dancing.
2: Make sure your MC knows that you want to do this and is fully prepared to help direct it properly.
3: You might want to request video footage from previous events so you can see how skilled your MC is when presenting these ideas.
4: Be candid with your MC about your feelings on using group participation dances to jump start the open dancing.
5: Make a list of no more than 15 "must play" dancing requests, but give the MC input on all of your dancing music preferences.
6: Make a list for your MC of "never play" songs that you absolutely do not want played at your reception, regardless of who might be requesting them.

CHAPTER 25

THE LAST DANCE

All good things must eventually come to an end. The same is true for every great reception celebration. The big question is…will your ending be forgettable or unforgettable? Will your guests leave with glowing comments of praise, raving about the enjoyable time that was had by all? Will they filter out little by little as the party goes later and later into the night? Will the majority of them join you for one last dance before you head off to your honeymoon? Will your last dance be a fast-paced song that holds special memories for you and your small group of college friends that have stayed until the very end? There is no wrong or right answer to any of these questions. Only you can determine what kind of ending will best fit your wedding reception celebration. In this chapter, we'll go over a few options for making your last dance into an ending that will bring closure to your party in a truly memorable way.

Leave Them Wanting Just a Little More ★★★★

When your reception comes to a close, if your guests begin to "boo" or they start chanting "one more song," then it's a pretty safe bet that your entertainment vendors have done a tremendous job. There is a reason why most movies don't go longer than 2 hours. The same could be said for the average length of concerts. Knowing "when to say when" is one of the most important aspects of creating good entertainment. If you choose to end your reception a little earlier than originally planned because you want to end things on a high note (and perhaps you are both already getting worn out), you will be joined during your last dance by a larger percentage of your guests and your ending will be truly memorable for all of them. One couple at a Sunday evening wedding in September of 2005 told me they were pretty sure their guests would not even dance at their reception. After getting the entire group dancing to about 5 songs in a row, they asked to begin the last dance an hour earlier than their location required the party to end. They opted for the early ending because they wanted to end on a high note, and they couldn't imagine anything topping the unexpected, yet energetic, dancing.

The Circle of Love ★★★/★★★★★

Have the MC invite everyone to make a big circle around both of you during your last dance. Getting everyone involved in this moment not only makes it more memorable for them, but it can also result in some

fantastic photos of the two of you surrounded by all your friends and family in the closing moments of your celebration. Your MC may have some special methods for making this into a 5 star event, but don't spoil the surprise by asking.

"Best Wishes" from the Circle of Love ★★★★

Building on the Circle of Love idea, Randy Bartlett, a nationally known wedding entertainer based out of Sacramento, CA, says, *"Have your MC move quickly around the circle of guests during your last dance letting each of them express their best wishes to both of you on the microphone. Your MC will most likely need an assistant to keep the music running."*[1]

Say Your "Goodbyes" from the Circle of Love ★★★★

Building on the Circle of Love idea, move around the circle bidding farewell and expressing your appreciation to each person that has remained until the end of your reception. Depending on the size of your group, you may want to select more than one song for this last dance.

Invite Your Guests to Make a Big Mess! ★★★★

Andy Austin, a popular wedding entertainer from Dallas/Forth Worth, TX, says, *"Have your MC hand your guests confetti sticks and streamers that can be used during your last dance to create an ending that looks like a paper factory just exploded at your reception! Just make sure to clear this idea in advance with the staff at your location."*[2]

Top 10 Last Dance Music Suggestions:
"Closing Time" *by Semisonic*
"Goodnight Sweetheart" *by The Spaniels*
"Good Riddance (Time of Your Life)" *by Green Day*
"The Last Dance" *by Frank Sinatra*
"Last Dance" *by Donna Summer*
"The Time Of My Life" *by Jennifer Warnes & Bill Medley*
"Two Tickets To Paradise" *by Eddie Money*
"Unforgettable" *by Natalie Cole & Nat King Cole*
"Wonderful Tonight" *by Eric Clapton*
"You'll Accomp'ny Me" *by Bob Seger*

BRIAN & JENNIFER

May 6th, 2006

Silverado Canyon, California

The Formal Toasts on Instant Replay

The Formal Toasts presented by Jennifer's Parents, along with both Best Men, and the Matron & Maid of Honor were very well done. With some quick editing, a few of the most poignant and humorous comments (which had been recorded) were "mixed" into the song, "Wonderful Tonight," which had been Brian & Jennifer's selection for their Last Dance. As they were surrounded by their guests, everyone was amazed to hear the toasts replaying, creating an unforgettable moment.

*Video Montage

Just days before their wedding, Brian & Jennifer found themselves in a minor crisis. Apparently, the wrong songs had been used in their Video Montage DVD. With a little rehearsal, to get the timing down, we were able to mix the correct songs live on the spot. The guests never even knew.

RECEPTION AGENDA

6:00
Grand Entrance
"Beautiful Day" *by U2*
6:15-7:20
Toasts & Dinner
7:25
Special Dances
First Dance
"After All"
by Cher & Peter Cetera
Father/Daughter Dance
"Butterfly Kisses"
by Bob Carlisle
Mother/Son Dance
"The Way You Look Tonight"
by Frank Sinatra
Wedding Party Dance
"We Are Family"
by Sister Sledge
7:40-8:05
Open Dancing
8:05
Longevity Dance
"Let's Stay Together"
by Al Green
8:10
Cake Cutting
"Sugar, Sugar"
by The Archies
"This Magic Moment"
by The Drifters
8:20
Video Montage*
8:35
Bouquet & Garter Toss
"Independent Woman"
by Destiny's Child
"Lady Marmalade"
from Moulin Rouge Sdtk
"I Melt With You"
by Modern English
"Start Me Up"
by The Rolling Stones
8:45-9:55
Open Dancing
Last Dance
"Unforgettable"
by Nat King Cole
"Wonderful Tonight"
by Eric Clapton

BRIAN & JENNIFER

177

CHAPTER 26

THE BIG SENDOFF

When your last dance has ended you can say goodbye to your guests, one at a time, or you can wave to all of them at the same time as they give you a sendoff to remember. Your reception can and should be an enjoyable, memorable, and entertaining celebration. When and how you do your last dance is primarily about providing closure for your guests. Having a big sendoff will help to solidify those feelings, but more importantly, it will also serve as the final chapter of your own memories. This choice is completely up to you. Do you want the final mental images of your reception to be of loading up your presents and watching as your decorations are taken down? Or, would you like to run to your waiting limousine as your guests are cheering your departure? In this chapter, we'll wrap up with a few unique ways to exit your celebration that will be simply unforgettable.

The Human Tunnel Exit ★★★

If your options for a memorable exit are limited, or you just want keep things simple, have your MC instruct your guests to form two lines facing each other, starting from the exit doors back to the dance floor. When the guests are all in position, they'll be instructed to raise their arms over the opening between them forming a human tunnel. Then, you will both race though the tunnel as your guests cheer your departure.

The Petal Toss Exit ★★★

Have the catering staff, or your coordinator, provide your guests with paper cones filled with flower petals as they head outside to prepare for your exit. The MC will keep you inside until everyone is in position. Then, the two of you will race outside as the guests shower you with flower petals and adulation.

The Bubbles Exit ★★★

Have the catering staff, or your coordinator, provide your guests with mini bottle of bubbles as they head outside to prepare for your exit. The MC will keep you inside until everyone is in position and the bubbles have filled a large enough volume of space for your dramatic exit. Then, the two of you will race outside as the guests greet you cheering as you dash through a cloud of bubbles on your way to your transportation.

The Sparkler Exit ★★★

Have the catering staff, or your coordinator, provide your guests with sparklers and lighters as they head outside to prepare for your exit. The MC will keep you inside until everyone is in position and their sparklers are all lit. Then, the two of you will race outside as the guests begin to cheer and wave their sparklers in the air. Always check this out with your reception location in advance due to possible fire hazard issues. And it's always wise to test your sparklers before buying a large quantity, to see which ones will last the longest and give off the least amount of smoke.

The Paparazzi Exit ★★★

Have the catering staff, or your coordinator, provide your guests with disposable cameras as they head outside to prepare for your exit. Have the MC encourage those with their own flash cameras to bring them outside as well. The MC will keep you inside until everyone is in position. Then, the two of you will race outside as the guests greet you like a rabid throng of paparazzi photographers trying to capture photos of a celebrity power couple arriving for a movie premiere.

The Surprise Running Exit ★★★★

Randy Bartlett, a nationally known wedding entertainer based out of Sacramento, CA, says, *"Work with your MC ahead of time to prepare a surprise for your guests that will take place right after your last dance has finished. When the song has ended, your MC will ask (over the microphone) where the two of you are going on your honeymoon, and as soon as you shout back your answer...you both make a mad dash for the exit! This can be a great idea if you have a flight to catch and really do need to make a fast getaway. Just be sure your goodbyes have been completed before your last dance begins."[1]*

SOME HELPFUL SUGGESTIONS
1: Your location should be consulted if you want to create a big sendoff. There may be local noise ordinances that prohibit them.
2: This would be a great moment to capture on film or video. However, if your photographer or videographer has already departed, consider arranging for someone else to take some photos and/or video footage of your exit.
3: Make sure your MC knows that you want to do this and is fully prepared to help direct it properly.
4: You may want to change into your departure outfits before your exit, or you may prefer to leave in your wedding attire. Either way, make arrangements to have someone pack your bags in your transportation for you before making this dramatic exit.

conclusion

Decades ago, when mobile disc jockeys first came on the scene and began competing with bands for wedding reception bookings, the primary benefit being offered by both was fun music for open dancing. Ever since, the wedding magazine editors and the authors of bridal planning books have been unwittingly short-changing their readers by only discussing music selections, instead of the necessary ingredients for creating entertaining receptions. This oversight certainly wasn't intentional. Until recently, the vast majority of wedding entertainment vendors had only promoted themselves as "music" for dancing.

But in the last few years, there has been a major shift in the world of wedding entertainment. Recognizing the increasing trends among brides and the general public to create their own style in everything they do, many wedding entertainers began finding ways to offer the same level of personalization for the various entertainment choices involved in creating fun receptions. Not that long ago, your options with a cup of coffee were typically cream and sugar. Today's bride can go into any Starbucks Coffee® and order her own personalized drink from 55,000 drink options[1]. Resources like TheKnot.com have created unprecedented opportunities for brides to compare notes on their wedding plans. Creative options for personalizing the dresses, decorations, photos, appetizers, beverages, and the vows have become all the rage.

But the primary reason why the entertainment aspects of wedding receptions have remained unreported for so long can be attributed to the photo rich, décor focused, production oriented presentations that are currently selling the image over the experience. Today's brides are being touted for creating unique centerpieces and seating cards because those items are easy to display in living color on a glossy page. It's not nearly as easy to showcase images of a grand entrance that has everyone in stitches while expecting the reader to understand the context and uniqueness of the moment that was created. What photo could communicate the overwhelming emotion a bride might be feeling the moment she hears a special surprise phone message from her beloved grandmother who was too sick to attend the wedding? It would certainly be possible to capture her emotional facial reactions with a moving snapshot. But the reader would never be able to connect her reaction to the experience itself, without the benefit of being there or hearing the actual recording. This has created what I like to refer to as a "blind spot" of valuable information that brides need to know, but have not yet been given....until now.

"The Best Wedding Reception...Ever!" has been written as guide for every bride (and groom) who will be preparing for their wedding reception and may be seriously concerned about whether or not their guests will have an enjoyable time. According to a 2006 survey promoted by the Association of Bridal Consultants (ABC) and taken by the readers of Brides Magazine, "39% of the brides who responded said one of their 'top worries' was 'not having a fun reception,' topped only by 'going over budget' at 65%, and 'forgetting a crucial detail' at 50%."[2] It is my conviction and belief that no bride should ever have to hope that her reception will actually be fun.

Seeing a real need for accurate information that can help brides and grooms create and experience truly entertaining receptions, I developed a seminar on creating entertaining receptions in July of 1999. The notes from that seminar were soon turned into a small, 22 page booklet which was distributed on a very limited basis. As I would visit the wedding planning section in the bookstores and read the bridal magazines year after year, I kept thinking that the information presented in that 22 page booklet needed to be expanded and given as a gift to each bride who truly wanted a fun celebration on her wedding day. Now, 7 long years later, that dream has become reality. My fulfillment in completing this book will only be surpassed by the reports I expect to hear from you, the reader, about how the information that has been presented in these pages helped you to create an event that is still being lauded to this day by your friends and family as "The Best Wedding Reception...Ever!"

Have fun,

Peter Merry

Peter Merry
"The Fun Wedding Guy!"

P.S. I sincerely welcome and invite any and all feedback about this book. My e-mail address is: Peter@TheBestWeddingReceptionEver.com

For additional information on any of the subjects covered in this book, please feel free to visit these web sites:

TheBestWeddingReceptionEver.com
WeddingEntertainmentDirector.com
MerryWeddings.com
PeterMerry.com
WEDGuild.com

THE END

bibliography

Chapter 2

1: DiscJockeyAmerica.com poll survey results. (Actual figure 85.5%)
Retrieved October 5th, 2004, from DiscJockeyAmerica.com website:
http://www.discjockeyamerica.com
2: St. Louis Bride & Groom Magazine of July 2003 page 106
3: Mark Ferrell in "Getting What You're Worth" seminar presented at the
Mobile Beat DJ Show on February 22nd, 2000.
Mark Ferrell can be contacted for more information via his web site:
http://www.discjockeyamerica.com
4: St. Louis Bride & Groom Magazine of July 2003 page 106

Chapter 7

1: Rev. Clint Hufft in "Create Your Perfect Wedding Ceremony!" seminar
presented on May 26th, 2004. Rev. Clint Hufft can be contacted for more
information via his web site: http://www.reverendclint.com
2: "iPod: The New Wedding DJ" by Derek John.
Featured on National Public Radio's broadcast on August 17th, 2005.
http://www.npr.org/templates/story/story.php?storyId=4803824
3: "It's a nice day for an iPod Wedding" by Alorie Gilbert.
Published on CNET News.com on September 20th, 2005.
http://news.com.com/lts+a+nice+day+for+an+iPod+wedding/2100-
1041_3-5874790.html
4: "The do-it-yourself wedding soundtrack" by Angel Rozas
Published in the Chicago Tribune on August 13th, 2006.
http://www.chicagotribune.com/news/opinion/chi-
0608130210aug13,0,3286908.story?coll=chi-newsopinionperspective-
hed (link no longer active)
5: "More couples program iPods for wedding music" by Raymond
Flandez Published in the Wall Street Journal on August 24th, 2006.
http://www.post-gazette.com/pg/06236/716012-96.stm
6: "25 Tips You'll Never Find in a Bridal Magazine" by Erinn Bucklan
Published in Cosmopolitan Magazine, June 2004, Page 203.
7: "Chat Rash 010" hosted by Bill James.
Published on dajradio.com August 31st, 2006.
http://www.djaradio.com/?p=121
8: DJ Times 2004 Comprehensive DJ Market Survey
Retrieved January 29, 2007, from DJTimes.com web site:
http://www.djtimes.com/advertiser_info/media/djt04_market_survey.pdf

Chapter 8

1: Producer. (n.d.). *Dictionary.com Unabridged (v 1.1).*
Retrieved January 23, 2007, from Dictionary.com website:
http://dictionary.reference.com/browse/Producer

2: Coordinator. Retrieved January 23, 2007, from Encarta.msn.com
website: http://encarta.msn.com/dictionary_/Coordinator.html

3: Master of Ceremonies. (n.d.). *Dictionary.com Unabridged (v 1.1).*
Retrieved January 23, 2007, from Dictionary.com website:
http://dictionary.reference.com/browse/Master of Ceremonies

4: Director. (n.d.). *Dictionary.com Unabridged (v 1.1).*
Retrieved January 23, 2007, from Dictionary.com website:
http://dictionary.reference.com/browse/Director

Chapter 12

1: John Lennon, "Beautiful Boy" from album "Double Fantasy" 1980
Retrieved January 27, 2007, from Wikiquote.org website:
http://en.wikiquote.org/wiki/John_Lennon

Chapter 15

1: Jim Cerone submitted this idea. Jim Cerone can be contacted for more
information via his web site: http://www.jimcerone.com

Chapter 16

1: Scott Faver submitted this idea. Scott Faver can be contacted for more
information via his web site: http://www.thepartyfavers.com

2: Andy Austin submitted this idea. Andy Austin can be contacted for
more information via his web site: http://www.litedallas.com

Chapter 17

1: Tom Haibeck is the author of "Wedding Toasts Made Easy" and
"The Wedding MC." Tom Haibeck can be contacted for more information
via his web site: http://www.weddingtoasts.com

2: Randy Bartlett submitted this idea. Randy Bartlett can be contacted for
more information via his web site: http://www.premierentertainment.biz

Chapter 18

1: Ben Miller submitted this idea. Ben Miller can be contacted for more
information via his web site: http://www.thepremierentertainment.com

2: Jim & Denise Sanchez submitted this idea. They can be contacted for
more information via their web site: http://www.aceweddings.com

3: Curtis Hoekstra submitted this idea. Curtis Hoekstra can be contacted
for more information via his web site:
http://www.remarkablereceptions.com

4: Randy Bartlett submitted this idea. Randy Bartlett can be contacted for
more information via his web site: http://www.premierentertainment.biz

5: James Loram submitted this idea. James Loram can be contacted for
more information via his web site: http://www.lastdance.net

Chapter 19

1: Ben Miller submitted this idea. Ben Miller can be contacted for more
information via his web site: http://www.thepremierentertainment.com

2: Jorge Lopez submitted this idea. Jorge Lopez can be contacted for
more information via his web site: http://www.jandmentertainment.com

3: "First Dance on the Clouds"
Retrieved February 2, 2007, from J & M Entertainment, Inc. website:
http://www.uxtm.com/demos/JM/Michele-Angel-wedding.html

4: "Wedding First Dance with a Twist"
Retrieved February 2, 2007, from YouTube.com website:
http://www.youtube.com/watch?v=6qd_j98-y-M&NR

Chapter 20

1: Bill Hermann submitted this idea. Bill Hermann can be contacted for more information via his web site: http://www.bluechipdj.com

Chapter 21

1: Ron Ruth submitted this idea. Ron Ruth can be contacted for more information via his web site: http://www.ronruthweddings.com

2: Bill Hermann submitted this idea. Bill Hermann can be contacted for more information via his web site: http://www.bluechipdj.com

3: Bill Hermann submitted this idea. Bill Hermann can be contacted for more information via his web site: http://www.bluechipdj.com

4: Ben Miller submitted this idea. Ben Miller can be contacted for more information via his web site: http://www.thepremierentertainment.com

Chapter 22

1: Greg Lowder submitted this idea. Greg Lowder can be contacted for more information via his web site: http://www.djseattle.com

2: Randy Bartlett submitted this idea. Randy Bartlett can be contacted for more information via his web site: http://www.premierentertainment.biz

3: Alex Tamas submitted this idea. Alex Tamas can be contacted for more information via his web site: http://alexandersmusicservice.com

Chapter 23

1: Jim & Denise Sanchez submitted this idea. They can be contacted for more information via their web site: http://www.aceweddings.com

1: Randy Bartlett submitted this idea. Randy Bartlett can be contacted for more information via his web site: http://www.premierentertainment.biz

3: "Wedding Party Thriller"
Retrieved February 2, 2007, from YouTube.com website:
http://www.youtube.com/watch?v=OPmYbP0F4Zw&eurl=

4: "Dance For My Sister's Wedding"
Retrieved February 6, 2007, from YouTube.com website:
http://www.youtube.com/watch?v=uojhahf7lo4

5: Andy Austin submitted this idea. Andy Austin can be contacted for more information via his web site: http://www.litedallas.com

6: Mark & Rebecca Ferrell submitted this idea. They can be contacted for more information via their web site: http://www.discjockeyamerica.com

7: Carl Young submitted this idea. Carl Young can be contacted for more information via his web site: http://www.1stchoicevideo.net

8: Mike Colón submitted this idea. Mike Colón can be contacted for more information via his web site: http://www.mikecolon.com

Chapter 24

1: Bill James McElree submitted this idea. Bill James McElree can be contacted for more information via e-mail: mcelreb@hotmail.com

Chapter 25

1: Randy Bartlett submitted this idea. Randy Bartlett can be contacted for more information via his web site: http://www.premierentertainment.biz

2: Andy Austin submitted this idea. Andy Austin can be contacted for more information via his web site: http://www.litedallas.com

Chapter 26

1: Randy Bartlett submitted this idea. Randy Bartlett can be contacted for more information via his web site: http://www.premierentertainment.biz

Bibliography

Conclusion

1: "The Star Of Starbucks" reported by Scott Pelley, produced by
Tom Anderson for "60 Minutes." Broadcast on CBS News April 23, 2006.
2: Association of Bridal Consultants (ABC) from
2006 Brides Magazine readers survey.
Retrieved February 4, 2007, from SignOnSanDiego.com website:
http://www.signonsandiego.com/weddings/advice/stories.php?StoryID=18

The Wedding Entertainment Director™ logo included on page 72 is the trademarked property of the Wedding Entertainment Directors Guild™, as is all public use of the term Wedding Entertainment Director™, both of which have been included in this book with permission.
For more information on the Wedding Entertainment Directors Guild™, visit their web site: http://www.wedguild.com

The contents listed in this Bibliography can also be found on the web site for the book, with active hyperlinks. Just visit:
http://www.TheBestWeddingReceptionEver.com

If you have a creative wedding entertainment idea, or a story of a uniquely entertaining moment that occurred at a wedding reception, please feel free to send in any submissions to be considered for future editions of this book. All submissions will be given consideration and any the author selects to include will be cited and referenced in this Bibliography with a web address, e-mail or other preferred contact information. Please e-mail all submissions to:

FunIdeas@TheBestWeddingReceptionEver.com

Bibliography

photo credits

I will remain eternally grateful for the amazing images provided by the following photographers, along with my former clients who have graciously allowed me the privilege of using their photographs:

Jim Kennedy with Jim Kennedy Photography
http://www.jimkennedyphotography.com
(800) 264-4558

All photos on the Front and Back Cover including Peter's head shot.
Page: 193

Brian & Jennifer Varca
May 6th, 2006
Front & Back Cover
Pages: ii, 2, 4, 6, 20, 22, 26, 28, 31, 34, 36, 38, 62, 76, 116, 118, 119, 126, 128, 129, 132, 134, 135, 170, 172, 173, 177

Anderson & Maggie Hinsch
October 28th, 2006
Pages: 12, 40, 42, 105, 122, 124

Pete & Nichole Winfield
July 30th, 2005
Pages: 19, 98, 100

Jared Bauman with Bauman Photography
http://www.jbaumanphoto.com
(619) 232-3020

Brent & Elana Redd
August 26th, 2006
Pages: 8, 9, 97, 158, 160

Mike Colón with Mike Colón Photography
http://www.mikecolon.com
(800) 992-6650

Pages: 14, 16, 84, 136, 138

Thomas & Emmy Antunez
July 16th, 2004
Pages 44, 46

Jason & Susan Lai
February 22nd, 2003
Pages: 78, 80, 110, 112

Becker with Becker Photographer
http://www.thebecker.com
(800) 675-3050

Garrett & Amy Pendergraft
November 23rd, 2002
Page: 25

Todd & Rebekah Ghilarducci
June 26th, 1999
Pages: 150, 152

Mike Gillmore with Mike Gillmore Photography
http://www.mikegillmorephotography.com
(949) 454-0676

Jason & Ashlee Hart
August 20th, 2006
Pages: 54, 83, 162

Gerry & Amber Prieto
June 19th, 2004
Pages: 72, 73, 164, 166

Todd & Keri Prochnow
September 30th, 2000
Pages: 144, 146

Eric & Rebecca Wilhoit
January 8th, 2006
Page: 148, 149

Matt & Jamie Runyon
February 13th, 2005
Pages: 178, 180

Photo Credits

190

Megan Gentile with Megan Gentile Photography
http://www.megangentile.com
(415) 317-3431

Evan & Christine Lash
July 16th, 2005
Pages: 39, 92, 94

Julie Diebolt Price with Julie Diebolt Price Photography
http://www.jdpphotography.com
(714) 669-4537

Travis & Tina Baron
June 2nd, 2001
Page: 57

Aaron Delesie with Aaron Delesie Photographer
http://www.aarondelesie.com
(949) 378-9121

Dave & Sarah Nelson
July 3rd, 2005
Page: 65

Todd & Colleen Spencer
April 16th, 2005
Pages: 86, 88

Jared & Barbara Shideler
March 6th, 2005
Pages: 154, 156

Julie Weaver with Julie Weaver Photography
http://www.julieweaverphotography.com
(800) 363-7144

Eric & Julie Shute
October 15th, 2006
Page: 97, 103, 131, 140, 141, 169

Nicole Caldwell with Nicole Caldwell Photography
http://www.nicolecaldwell.com
(949) 433-9897

Jeff & Victoria Wisot
May 30th, 2004
Page: 91

Bob Stambach with Bob Stambach Photography
http://www.bobstambachphotography.com
(602) 993-4444

Curtis & Amy Hoekstra
March 3rd, 2005
Pages: 106, 108, 109, 163

Victor Sizemore with VCS Photography
http://www.vcsphoto.com
(800) 733-5060

Jake & Amanda Jerome
July 23rd, 2005
Page: 114

Dave Katinsky with Vision Masters Photography
http://www.visionmaster.com
(973) 808-6466

Mark Pedalino & Melissa Churchwell
August 5th, 2005
Pages: 121, 174, 176

Amanda Collins with Mandy Marie Photographer
http://www.mandymariephoto.com
(949) 280-1143

Chuck & Heidi Herchelroath
July 18th, 2004
Page: 181

Page 33 features Room Layout Diagrams designed by the author.

Page 69 features 3 anonymous photo submissions of DJ set-ups, and 2 which were submitted with permission by the owners. From top to bottom:
1: "How Many Watts?" was submitted anonymously
2: "Pretty Flashy?!" was submitted anonymously
3: "We've Got The Tools!" was submitted anonymously
4: "The BOSE® L1™...Nice!" was submitted by Bob Carpenter of Main Event Weddings in Greenville, RI. To contact Bob Carpenter for more information, please visit his web site: http://www.maineventweddings.com For more information on the BOSE® L1™ Cylindrical Radiator® System, visit the BOSE® web site: http://www.BOSE.com/controller?event=VIEW_ PRODUCT_ PAGE_EVENT&product=l1_single_live_music
5: "Finely Furnished!" was submitted by Andy Austin of Lite Dallas in Dallas/Forth Worth, TX. To contact Andy Austin for more information, please visit his web site: http://www.litedallas.com

about the author

Peter Merry has been helping couples create fun and entertaining wedding receptions since 1992. He has presented seminars on wedding entertainment performance techniques, wedding marketing, sales consultation skills, and the value of solid standards and ethics in business. These seminars have been presented to wedding entertainers in over 40 cities across the United States.

He has also frequently been asked to speak locally and nationally for various professional associations and conferences, including: ABC (Association of Bridal Consultants), ISES (International Special Events Society), NACE (National Association of Catering Executives), WMBA (Wedding Merchants Business Academy), and AFWPI (Association For Wedding Professionals International). He served as the 2003 and 2004 National ADJA President (American Disc Jockey Association).

He currently serves his clients as their Wedding Entertainment Director™ via his exclusive entertainment company, Merry Weddings, Inc. His varied entertainment background includes years of public speaking and teaching classes at Saddleback Church, serving as a "Morning Host" for KBRT AM 740, hosting and engineering his own Talk Radio Show on KBRT, and performing Stand-Up Comedy at the Improv.

He was born and raised in Seattle, Washington. He currently lives in Ladera Ranch, California with his wife Lisa. And, he is the proud step-father of Eric & Jason Lovato.

Peter's infectious passion for creating memorable moments at weddings has caused many to affectionately refer to him as "the fun wedding guy!" To learn more, visit his personal web site: PeterMerry.com.